Building Modern Web Applications with the MERN Stack

An Introduction for Beginners

October 2024

Dr Alex Bugeja, PhD

Table of Contents

Introduction

Welcome to the exciting world of web development! If you're reading this, you're likely eager to learn how to build modern, dynamic web applications using the powerful MERN stack. This book is designed as your guide, taking you from beginner to confident MERN developer, step by step. We'll explore each component of the stack, learn how they work together, and build practical projects to solidify your understanding.

What is the MERN Stack?

The MERN stack is a popular combination of technologies used to build full-stack web applications. "Full-stack" means that you're involved in building both the front-end (what the user sees and interacts with) and the back-end (the behind-the-scenes logic and data management). MERN stands for:

- **MongoDB:** A NoSQL database that stores your application's data in a flexible, document-oriented format (JSON-like). Think of it as a highly organized and efficient way to manage information.

- **Express.js:** A minimalist and flexible Node.js web application framework. It provides a simple and robust foundation for building APIs (Application Programming Interfaces), which act as the bridge between your front-end and back-end.

- **React.js:** A JavaScript library developed by Facebook for building user interfaces. React is known for its component-based architecture, which allows you to create reusable UI elements and manage the flow of data efficiently.

- **Node.js:** A JavaScript runtime environment that allows you to run JavaScript code outside of a web browser. This means you can use JavaScript to build server-side applications, command-line tools, and much more.

Why Choose the MERN Stack?

There are several reasons why the MERN stack has become a favorite among developers:

- **JavaScript Everywhere:** You use JavaScript throughout the entire development process, from the front-end to the back-end and even the database (MongoDB uses a JavaScript-like query language). This eliminates the need to switch between different languages and simplifies development.

- **Open Source and Free:** All the components of the MERN stack are open-source and free to use, making it a cost-effective choice for both individuals and businesses.

- **Large and Active Community:** A vast and active community surrounds the MERN stack. This means you'll find plenty of resources, tutorials, and support when you need it.

- **Flexibility and Scalability:** The MERN stack is known for its flexibility and scalability, allowing you to build applications ranging from small personal projects to large, enterprise-level systems.

- **Modern and Efficient:** The technologies in the MERN stack are modern and designed for efficient web development. React's component-based approach promotes code reusability, and Node.js's non-blocking architecture enables high performance.

Who Should Read This Book?

This book is perfect for you if:

- You're a beginner to web development and want to learn how to build full-stack applications.

- You have some basic programming experience (preferably with JavaScript) and are eager to explore the MERN stack.

- You're looking for a clear, concise, and practical guide to building modern web applications.

What You'll Learn

Throughout this book, we'll cover a wide range of topics, including:

- Setting up your development environment.

- Understanding the fundamentals of Node.js, Express.js, MongoDB, and React.

- Building RESTful APIs to handle data communication between the front-end and back-end.

- Creating dynamic and interactive user interfaces with React.

- Managing application state with React hooks and Redux.

- Implementing user authentication and authorization.

- Deploying your MERN stack application to the web.

- And much more!

Getting Started

Before you dive into the chapters, make sure you have a basic understanding of HTML, CSS, and JavaScript. These are the foundational building blocks of web development. If you're new to these technologies, there are many excellent online resources available to help you get up to speed.

We'll guide you through the installation and setup of all the necessary tools and software as we progress through the book. Don't worry if you're not familiar with them yet; we'll explain everything clearly and concisely.

Most importantly, approach this journey with a sense of curiosity and a willingness to learn. Web development is a constantly evolving field, and the best way to master it is to embrace the process of continuous learning and experimentation.

Now, let's get started on building amazing web applications with the MERN stack!

Chapter One: Understanding the MERN Stack

In the introduction, we briefly touched upon the individual components that make up the MERN stack. In this chapter, we'll dive deeper into each of these technologies, exploring their core concepts, strengths, and how they fit into the bigger picture of building a full-stack web application. By the end of this chapter, you'll have a solid foundational understanding of what each part of the MERN stack does and how they work together harmoniously.

MongoDB: Your Data's Home

At the heart of any application lies the data it manages. Whether it's user profiles, product information, or blog posts, your application needs a reliable and efficient way to store and retrieve this data. That's where MongoDB comes in.

MongoDB is a NoSQL database, which means it doesn't follow the traditional relational database model (like SQL databases). Instead of storing data in tables with rows and columns, MongoDB uses a document-oriented approach. Data is stored in flexible, JSON-like documents, making it well-suited for handling diverse and evolving data structures.

Think of a MongoDB database as a library. Each book in the library represents a document, and each document can have different fields (like title, author, and publication date). You can easily add new fields to a document without affecting other documents, providing a high degree of flexibility.

MongoDB's document-oriented nature offers several advantages:

- **Schema Flexibility:** You don't need to define a rigid schema upfront, allowing your data structure to evolve as your application's needs change.

- **Scalability:** MongoDB is designed to scale horizontally, meaning you can easily distribute your data across multiple servers to handle increasing loads.

- **High Performance:** MongoDB's use of documents and indexes allows for fast data retrieval, making it suitable for applications that require quick response times.

- **Easy to Use:** MongoDB provides a simple and intuitive query language for interacting with your data, making it easy to learn and use.

In the context of a MERN application, MongoDB typically serves as the back-end database. Your Express.js server will interact with MongoDB to store, retrieve, update, and delete data as needed.

Express.js: The Back-End Framework

While MongoDB handles the storage of your application's data, you need a way to manage the logic and interactions between your front-end and back-end. That's where Express.js comes into play.

Express.js is a Node.js web application framework. It provides a set of tools and features that simplify the process of building web servers and APIs. Think of it as a toolbox that gives you everything you need to create the back-end of your application.

Express.js is built on top of Node.js, which allows you to run JavaScript on the server-side. This means you can use the same language for both your front-end and back-end, streamlining the development process.

Express.js is known for its minimalism and flexibility. It doesn't impose a rigid structure or dictate how you should build your application. Instead, it gives you the freedom to choose the tools and libraries that best suit your needs.

Some key features of Express.js include:

- **Routing:** Easily define routes (URLs) and handle different HTTP requests (GET, POST, PUT, DELETE).

- **Middleware:** Add functionality to your application's request-response cycle, such as authentication, logging, and error handling.

- **Templating:** Render dynamic HTML pages using template engines like Handlebars or Pug.

- **API Development:** Easily create RESTful APIs to communicate with your front-end application.

In a MERN application, Express.js acts as the bridge between your front-end (React.js) and your database (MongoDB). It receives requests from the front-end, processes them, interacts with the database, and sends responses back to the front-end.

React.js: Building User Interfaces

While Express.js handles the back-end logic, React.js takes care of the front-end, the part of your application that users directly interact with.

React.js is a JavaScript library for building user interfaces (UIs). It's developed and maintained by Facebook and has become one of the most popular front-end libraries in recent years.

React.js is known for its component-based architecture. You build your UI by creating reusable components, each responsible for a specific part of the interface. Think of it like building with Lego blocks – you can combine and reuse components to create complex and dynamic UIs.

React.js uses a declarative approach, meaning you describe what you want your UI to look like, and React takes care of updating the UI based on changes in data or user interactions. This makes it easier to reason about your code and manage the complexity of your UI.

Some key features of React.js include:

- **JSX:** A syntax extension that allows you to write HTML-like code within your JavaScript.

- **Virtual DOM:** A lightweight representation of the actual DOM (Document Object Model) that React uses to efficiently update the UI.

- **Component Lifecycle:** Methods that allow you to control the behavior of your components at different stages of their lifecycle.

- **State Management:** Tools and techniques for managing the data that drives your UI.

In a MERN application, React.js is responsible for rendering the UI, handling user interactions, and communicating with the back-end (Express.js) to fetch and update data.

Node.js: The JavaScript Runtime

Both Express.js and React.js rely on Node.js, the JavaScript runtime environment. Node.js allows you to run JavaScript code outside of a web browser, on the server-side or as standalone applications.

Node.js uses a non-blocking, event-driven architecture, making it highly efficient for handling concurrent requests. This means it can handle a large number of requests simultaneously without slowing down.

Node.js has a vast ecosystem of modules and libraries that you can use to extend its functionality. This includes libraries for networking, file system access, database interaction, and much more.

In a MERN application, Node.js provides the runtime environment for both Express.js (on the back-end) and React.js (during development and build processes).

The MERN Stack in Action

Now that we've explored each component individually, let's see how they fit together in a typical MERN application:

- **User Interaction:** The user interacts with the React.js front-end, triggering an event (e.g., clicking a button).

- **Request to Back-End:** React.js sends a request to the Express.js back-end API.

- **Back-End Processing:** Express.js receives the request, processes it, and may interact with MongoDB to retrieve or update data.

- **Response to Front-End:** Express.js sends a response back to the React.js front-end, typically in JSON format.

- **UI Update:** React.js receives the response and updates the UI accordingly, reflecting the changes or data retrieved from the back-end.

This cycle of interactions continues as the user interacts with the application. The MERN stack provides a seamless flow of data and logic between the front-end and back-end, enabling you to build dynamic and interactive web applications.

Conclusion

Understanding the individual components of the MERN stack and how they interact is crucial for building successful web applications. MongoDB provides the data storage, Express.js handles the back-end logic and API, React.js builds the user interface, and Node.js provides the runtime environment. By mastering these technologies, you'll have the power to create modern, scalable, and efficient web applications that meet the demands of today's digital world.

Chapter Two: Setting Up Your Development Environment

Before we embark on our journey of building MERN applications, we need to set up a proper development environment on our computer. This involves installing the necessary software and tools that will enable us to write, test, and run our code. Think of it as preparing your workshop with all the essential tools before starting a woodworking project.

In this chapter, we'll guide you through the process of setting up your development environment, step-by-step. We'll cover the installation of Node.js and npm (Node Package Manager), MongoDB, a suitable code editor, and Git (for version control). Don't worry if these terms sound unfamiliar – we'll explain each one as we go along.

Installing Node.js and npm

Node.js is the JavaScript runtime environment that powers our back-end (Express.js) and is also essential for various front-end development tasks. npm, the Node Package Manager, comes bundled with Node.js and is used to manage packages (libraries and tools) that we'll need for our projects.

To install Node.js and npm, head over to the official Node.js website (https://nodejs.org) and download the installer for your operating system (Windows, macOS, or Linux). The website usually automatically detects your operating system and recommends the appropriate installer.

Once the download is complete, run the installer and follow the on-screen instructions. The installation process is generally straightforward and involves accepting the license agreement and choosing the installation location.

After the installation is finished, you can verify that Node.js and npm are installed correctly by opening your terminal or command prompt and running the following commands:

```
node -v

npm -v
```

These commands should display the installed versions of Node.js and npm, respectively. If you see the version numbers, you're good to go!

Installing MongoDB

MongoDB is the database we'll use to store our application's data. We have two options for installing MongoDB:

1. **Installing MongoDB Community Server:** This is the free and open-source version of MongoDB, suitable for development and learning purposes.

2. **Using MongoDB Atlas:** This is a cloud-based database service offered by MongoDB. It provides a managed MongoDB instance, eliminating the need for manual installation and configuration.

For this book, we'll focus on installing MongoDB Community Server, as it gives us more control over our database environment. To install it, visit the MongoDB download center (https://www.mongodb.com/try/download/community) and choose the installer for your operating system.

Follow the installation instructions specific to your operating system. You might need to add MongoDB to your system's PATH environment variable so that you can access it from the command line.

Once the installation is complete, you can start the MongoDB server by running the following command in your terminal or command prompt:

```
mongod
```

This command starts the MongoDB server and makes it listen for connections on the default port (27017). You can verify that the server is running by opening a new terminal or command prompt window and running the following command:

```
mongo
```

This command connects to the MongoDB server and opens the MongoDB shell, where you can interact with your database. You should see a message indicating that you've connected to the server.

Choosing a Code Editor

A good code editor is essential for writing and editing your code efficiently. There are many excellent code editors available, each with its strengths and weaknesses. Here are a few popular choices:

- **Visual Studio Code (VS Code):** A free and open-source editor developed by Microsoft. It's highly customizable and has a vast extension ecosystem.

- **Sublime Text:** A powerful and lightweight editor known for its speed and responsiveness.

- **Atom:** Another free and open-source editor developed by GitHub. It's highly customizable and has a strong community.

- **WebStorm:** A commercial editor specifically designed for web development. It offers advanced features like code completion and debugging tools.

The choice of a code editor is largely a matter of personal preference. We recommend trying out a few different editors and choosing the one that feels most comfortable and productive for you.

For this book, we'll use Visual Studio Code (VS Code) in our examples and screenshots. It's a popular choice among web developers and offers a good balance of features and ease of use.

Installing Git

Git is a version control system that allows you to track changes to your code over time and collaborate with others on projects. It's an essential tool for any developer, regardless of the technology stack they're using.

To install Git, visit the official Git website (https://git-scm.com/) and download the installer for your operating system. Follow the installation instructions specific to your operating system.

Once Git is installed, you can configure your Git username and email address using the following commands in your terminal or command prompt:

```
git config --global user.name "Your Name"

git config --global user.email
"your.email@example.com"
```

Replace "Your Name" and "your.email@example.com" with your actual name and email address.

Creating Your First Project

Now that we've installed all the necessary tools, let's create our first MERN project. Choose a directory where you want to store your project files and create a new folder for it. For example, you could create a folder named "my-mern-app" on your desktop.

Open your terminal or command prompt and navigate to the project folder using the `cd` command. For example:

```
cd ~/Desktop/my-mern-app
```

Now, let's initialize a new Node.js project using npm:

```
npm init -y
```

This command creates a `package.json` file in your project folder. This file stores metadata about your project, including its name, version, dependencies, and scripts.

Next, let's create two subfolders within our project folder: "client" for our React.js front-end code and "server" for our Express.js back-end code. You can create these folders using your file explorer or the following commands in your terminal:

```
mkdir client

mkdir server
```

Our project structure should now look like this:

my-mern-app/

- client/

- server/

- package.json

Conclusion

Setting up your development environment is a crucial first step in your MERN stack journey. We've covered the installation of Node.js and npm, MongoDB, a code editor, and Git. We've also created our first project folder and initialized a Node.js project.

With our environment ready, we can now move on to exploring the individual components of the MERN stack in more detail, starting with Node.js and Express.js in the next chapter.

Chapter Three: Introduction to Node.js and Express.js

In the previous chapter, we set up our development environment and laid the groundwork for our MERN stack journey. Now, it's time to delve into the back-end side of things, starting with Node.js and Express.js. These two technologies form the foundation of our server-side applications, handling everything from routing requests to interacting with the database.

Node.js: JavaScript Beyond the Browser

Traditionally, JavaScript was primarily used as a client-side scripting language, confined to the web browser. However, with the advent of Node.js, JavaScript broke free from these constraints and entered the realm of server-side programming. Node.js is a JavaScript runtime environment built on Chrome's V8 JavaScript engine, allowing you to execute JavaScript code outside the browser, on your computer or a server.

Node.js embraces an event-driven, non-blocking I/O model, making it highly efficient for handling concurrent requests. In simpler terms, it can juggle multiple tasks simultaneously without getting bogged down, unlike traditional blocking models that handle tasks one at a time. This efficiency is particularly crucial for web applications that need to respond swiftly to a multitude of user interactions.

Think of it like a restaurant with a single waiter (blocking model) versus one with multiple waiters (non-blocking model). In the first scenario, the waiter takes one order at a time, serves it, and then moves on to the next, potentially causing delays. In the second scenario, multiple waiters can take orders and serve customers concurrently, resulting in faster service.

Node.js has gained immense popularity in recent years, thanks to its speed, scalability, and the ability to use JavaScript for both front-end and back-end development. This "JavaScript everywhere" approach simplifies development and reduces the need to switch between different programming languages.

Exploring Node.js Modules

Node.js comes with a rich set of built-in modules that provide functionalities for various tasks, such as file system access, networking, and more. These modules are like pre-fabricated tools that you can readily use in your applications.

For instance, the `fs` (file system) module allows you to interact with files on your computer, enabling you to read, write, and manipulate files. The `http` module provides tools for creating web servers and handling HTTP requests and responses. The `os` module gives you information about the operating system, and so on.

To use a module, you simply need to `require` it in your JavaScript file. For example, to use the `fs` module, you would write:

```
const fs = require('fs');
```

This line of code imports the `fs` module and assigns it to the variable `fs`, allowing you to access its functions and properties.

npm: The Package Manager for Node.js

Besides the built-in modules, Node.js boasts a vast ecosystem of third-party packages, thanks to npm (Node Package Manager). npm is a command-line tool and online registry that makes it easy to discover, install, and manage packages created by other developers.

Imagine npm as a vast library where developers can share their tools and libraries. You can search for packages that fulfill specific needs, such as handling database interactions, processing images, or building user interfaces.

To install a package using npm, you use the `npm install` command followed by the package name. For example, to install the popular `express` package, you would run:

```
npm install express
```

This command downloads the `express` package and its dependencies and adds them to your project's `node_modules` folder.

npm also plays a crucial role in managing project dependencies. The `package.json` file in your project lists all the packages your project relies on, along with their versions. This ensures that when you share your project with others or deploy it to a server, the correct versions of the dependencies are installed.

Express.js: Simplifying Web Development

While Node.js provides the core functionalities for server-side JavaScript, Express.js builds upon it to offer a more streamlined and structured approach to web development. Express.js is a minimalist and flexible web application framework for Node.js. It provides a set of tools and conventions that make it easier to build web servers and APIs.

Think of Express.js as a scaffolding that provides a basic structure for your web application. It handles common tasks such as routing, middleware, and templating, allowing you to focus on the specific logic of your application.

Express.js is built around the concept of middleware. Middleware are functions that sit between your application and the incoming requests. They can intercept requests, modify them, perform actions, and pass them on to the next middleware or the final request handler.

This middleware architecture makes Express.js highly extensible and customizable. You can use middleware to handle tasks such as authentication, logging, error handling, and more.

Routing with Express.js

One of the core features of Express.js is routing. Routing determines how your application responds to different HTTP requests based on the requested URL. Express.js provides a simple and intuitive way to define routes and their corresponding handlers.

For example, to define a route that handles GET requests to the root URL ("/"), you would write:

```
const express = require('express');

const app = express();


app.get('/', (req, res) => {

  res.send('Hello from the root route!');

});
```

```
app.listen(3000, () => {

  console.log('Server listening on port
3000');

});
```

In this code snippet, we first require the `express` module and create an instance of the Express application. Then, we define a route for GET requests to "/" using `app.get()`. The second argument to `app.get()` is a callback function that handles the request. In this case, it simply sends the string "Hello from the root route!" as the response.

Finally, we start the server using `app.listen()`, specifying the port number (3000 in this case) on which the server will listen for incoming requests.

Middleware in Action

Let's illustrate the concept of middleware with a simple example. Suppose we want to log the timestamp of each incoming request. We can achieve this using a middleware function:

```
const express = require('express');

const app = express();


const requestLogger = (req, res, next) => {
```

```
    console.log(`Request received at: ${new
Date()}`);

    next();

};


app.use(requestLogger);


// Other routes and middleware


app.listen(3000, () => {

    console.log('Server listening on port
3000');

});
```

In this code, we define a middleware function called requestLogger. It takes three arguments: the request object (req), the response object (res), and the next function. Inside the function, we log the current timestamp and then call next().

The next() function is crucial in middleware. It signals to Express.js to move on to the next middleware in the chain or to the final request handler. If we don't call next(), the request will get stuck at this middleware.

We register the `requestLogger` middleware using `app.use()`. This means that the `requestLogger` function will be executed for every incoming request, regardless of the URL.

Handling Different HTTP Methods

Express.js provides methods for handling various HTTP methods, such as GET, POST, PUT, DELETE, and more. These methods correspond to different actions that a client can perform on a resource.

For example, a GET request is typically used to retrieve data, while a POST request is used to create new data. A PUT request is used to update existing data, and a DELETE request is used to delete data.

You can define routes for different HTTP methods using the corresponding methods on the app object. For example:

```
app.get('/users', (req, res) => {

  // Handle GET request to /users (e.g.,
retrieve list of users)

});
```

```
app.post('/users', (req, res) => {

  // Handle POST request to /users (e.g.,
create a new user)

});
```

```javascript
app.put('/users/:id', (req, res) => {

  // Handle PUT request to /users/:id (e.g.,
  update user with given ID)

});
```

```javascript
app.delete('/users/:id', (req, res) => {

  // Handle DELETE request to /users/:id
  (e.g., delete user with given ID)

});
```

In these examples, we define routes for GET, POST, PUT, and DELETE requests to the /users endpoint. The :id in the PUT and DELETE routes indicates a dynamic route parameter, which allows us to handle requests for specific users based on their ID.

Serving Static Files

Express.js makes it easy to serve static files, such as HTML, CSS, JavaScript, and images, from a specific directory. This is useful for serving the front-end assets of your application.

To serve static files from a directory, you use the express.static() middleware. For example, to serve files from the public directory, you would write:

```javascript
app.use(express.static('public'));
```

Now, if you have an `index.html` file in the `public` directory, you can access it by visiting the root URL of your application in the browser.

Templating with Express.js

Express.js supports various templating engines, such as Handlebars, Pug, and EJS, that allow you to generate dynamic HTML content on the server-side. Templating engines provide a way to embed dynamic data into HTML templates, making it easier to create customized web pages.

For instance, you can use a templating engine to generate a web page that displays a list of products retrieved from a database. The templating engine would take the product data and insert it into the HTML template, creating a dynamic web page that reflects the current data.

To use a templating engine with Express.js, you need to configure Express.js to use the desired engine and specify the directory where your templates are located.

Error Handling in Express.js

Error handling is an essential aspect of web application development. Express.js provides mechanisms for handling errors gracefully and providing informative error messages to users.

You can define error-handling middleware functions that catch errors that occur during request processing. These middleware functions typically take an error object as an argument and can perform actions such as logging the error, sending an error response to the client, or redirecting to an error page.

By implementing proper error handling, you can prevent your application from crashing and provide a better user experience.

Chapter Four: Building Your First Express.js Server

In the previous chapter, we introduced Node.js and Express.js, the dynamic duo that will power the back-end of our MERN stack applications. We explored Node.js's capabilities as a JavaScript runtime environment and Express.js's role as a minimalist web framework. Now, it's time to put this knowledge into practice and build our first Express.js server.

Creating the Server File

Let's start by creating a file where we'll write the code for our server. Navigate to the "server" folder we created in Chapter Two and create a new file named index.js. This file will serve as the entry point for our server-side application.

Open index.js in your code editor and let's begin by requiring the express module:

```
const express = require('express');
```

This line imports the express module and makes its functionalities available to us in our code.

Next, we'll create an instance of the Express application:

```
const app = express();
```

This creates an `app` object that represents our Express application. We'll use this object to define routes, configure middleware, and manage other aspects of our server.

Defining a Route

Now, let's define a simple route that handles GET requests to the root URL ("/"). We'll make this route respond with a "Hello from the server!" message.

```
app.get('/', (req, res) => {

  res.send('Hello from the server!');

});
```

In this code snippet, we use the `app.get()` method to define a route for GET requests to "/". The second argument to `app.get()` is a callback function that handles the request. This callback function takes two arguments: the request object (`req`) and the response object (`res`).

The `req` object represents the incoming request from the client and contains information such as the request headers, URL parameters, and request body. The `res` object represents the response that we'll send back to the client.

In our callback function, we use `res.send()` to send the string "Hello from the server!" as the response to the client.

Starting the Server

We've defined our route, but our server isn't running yet. To start the server, we need to tell it to listen on a specific port. Let's choose port 5000 for our server.

```
app.listen(5000, () => {

  console.log('Server listening on port
5000');

});
```

Here, we use `app.listen()` to start the server and make it listen on port 5000. The second argument to `app.listen()` is a callback function that will be executed once the server has started listening. In our callback function, we simply log a message to the console indicating that the server is running.

Testing the Server

Our server is now ready to handle requests. Let's test it out! Open your web browser and navigate to `http://localhost:5000`. You should see the "Hello from the server!" message displayed in your browser.

Congratulations! You've successfully built your first Express.js server. It's a simple server, but it demonstrates the fundamental concepts of Express.js routing and server setup.

Handling POST Requests

Let's expand our server's capabilities by adding a route that handles POST requests. POST requests are typically used to send data to the server, such as when submitting a form.

We'll define a route that handles POST requests to the "/data"
URL and simply logs the received data to the console.

```
app.post('/data', (req, res) => {

    console.log('Received data:', req.body);

    res.send('Data received!');

});
```

In this code snippet, we use `app.post()` to define a route for
POST requests to "/data". The callback function handles the
request and logs the received data to the console using
`console.log()`.

The `req.body` property contains the data sent in the request
body. To access this data, we need to use middleware that parses
the request body. We'll explore middleware in more detail later,
but for now, let's add the following middleware to our server:

```
const express = require('express');

const app = express();


// Middleware to parse JSON request bodies

app.use(express.json());
```

```
// ... (rest of the code)
```

This `express.json()` middleware parses incoming requests with JSON payloads and makes the parsed data available in `req.body`.

Now, if you send a POST request to `http://localhost:5000/data` with a JSON payload, the server will log the received data to the console and send back a "Data received!" message.

You can test this using tools like Postman or by writing a simple HTML form that submits data to this URL.

Serving Static Files

In many web applications, you need to serve static files, such as HTML, CSS, JavaScript, and images, to the client. Express.js makes it easy to serve static files from a specific directory.

Let's create a "public" folder in our server directory and add an `index.html` file to it. We'll then configure our server to serve files from this "public" folder.

```
const express = require('express');

const app = express();



// ... (other code)
```

```
// Serve static files from the 'public'
directory

app.use(express.static('public'));



// ... (rest of the code)
```

We use the `express.static()` middleware to serve files from the "public" directory. Now, if you navigate to `http://localhost:5000` in your browser, the server will serve the `index.html` file from the "public" folder.

Using Environment Variables

In real-world applications, you often need to store sensitive information, such as API keys or database credentials, outside of your code. This is where environment variables come in handy.

Environment variables are key-value pairs that are stored outside of your code and can be accessed by your application at runtime. This allows you to keep sensitive information separate from your codebase and configure your application for different environments (development, staging, production).

To use environment variables in your Express.js application, you can use the `process.env` object. For example, if you have an environment variable named `PORT`, you can access its value using `process.env.PORT`.

Let's modify our server to use an environment variable for the port number:

```javascript
const express = require('express');

const app = express();


// ... (other code)


const PORT = process.env.PORT || 5000; //
Use environment variable or default to 5000


app.listen(PORT, () => {

  console.log(`Server listening on port
${PORT}`);

});
```

In this code, we check if the PORT environment variable is
defined. If it is, we use its value; otherwise, we default to port
5000.

To set environment variables, you can use the command line or a
.env file. We'll explore these methods in more detail later.

Implementing Middleware

Middleware functions are a powerful feature of Express.js that
allow you to add custom logic to the request-response cycle.
Middleware functions can intercept requests, modify them,

perform actions, and pass them on to the next middleware or the final request handler.

Let's create a simple middleware function that logs the requested URL to the console:

```
const urlLogger = (req, res, next) => {

  console.log('Requested URL:', req.url);

  next();

};
```

This `urlLogger` middleware function takes three arguments: the request object (`req`), the response object (`res`), and the `next` function. Inside the function, we log the requested URL to the console and then call `next()`.

The `next()` function is crucial in middleware. It signals to Express.js to move on to the next middleware in the chain or to the final request handler. If we don't call `next()`, the request will get stuck at this middleware.

To use this middleware, we need to register it with our Express application using `app.use()`:

```
const express = require('express');

const app = express();
```

```
// ... (other code)


app.use(urlLogger); // Register the
urlLogger middleware


// ... (rest of the code)
```

Now, for every incoming request, the urlLogger middleware will be executed, logging the requested URL to the console before passing the request on to the next middleware or route handler.

Conclusion

In this chapter, we've built our first Express.js server from the ground up. We've explored fundamental concepts such as defining routes, handling different HTTP methods, serving static files, using environment variables, and implementing middleware.

With this foundation, we're well-equipped to move on to the next chapter, where we'll integrate MongoDB into our application and learn how to interact with our database using Mongoose.

Chapter Five: Working with MongoDB and Mongoose

In the previous chapters, we've built a solid foundation for our back-end using Node.js and Express.js. We've learned how to handle requests, define routes, and serve static files. Now, it's time to introduce the "M" in MERN: MongoDB, our database of choice. We'll explore MongoDB's document-oriented approach and learn how to interact with it seamlessly using Mongoose, an Object Data Modeling (ODM) library for Node.js.

MongoDB: A NoSQL Database for the Modern Web

MongoDB is a NoSQL database, which stands for "not only SQL." Unlike traditional relational databases that store data in tables with rows and columns, MongoDB adopts a document-oriented approach. It stores data in flexible, JSON-like documents, making it ideal for handling diverse and evolving data structures.

Think of a MongoDB database as a filing cabinet. Each drawer in the cabinet represents a collection, and each file within a drawer represents a document. Documents can have different fields, similar to how files can contain various pieces of information. You can easily add new fields to a document without affecting other documents, providing a high degree of flexibility.

MongoDB's document-oriented nature offers several advantages:

- **Schema flexibility:** You don't need to define a rigid schema upfront, allowing your data structure to adapt as your application's needs change.

- **Scalability:** MongoDB is designed to scale horizontally, meaning you can easily distribute your data across multiple servers to handle increasing loads.

- **High performance:** MongoDB's use of documents and indexes enables fast data retrieval, making it suitable for applications that demand quick response times.

- **Ease of use:** MongoDB provides a simple and intuitive query language for interacting with your data, making it easy to learn and use.

In the context of a MERN application, MongoDB typically serves as the back-end database. Your Express.js server will interact with MongoDB to store, retrieve, update, and delete data as needed.

Introducing Mongoose: Bridging the Gap

While you can interact with MongoDB directly using its native driver, Mongoose provides a higher-level abstraction that simplifies database interactions and adds structure to your data. Mongoose is an Object Data Modeling (ODM) library for Node.js and MongoDB.

Think of Mongoose as a translator between your Express.js application and MongoDB. It allows you to define schemas for your data, which act as blueprints for your documents. Schemas define the fields that a document can have, their data types, and any validation rules.

Mongoose also provides convenient methods for creating, reading, updating, and deleting documents, making database interactions more intuitive and less error-prone.

Installing Mongoose

Before we can start using Mongoose, we need to install it. Open your terminal or command prompt, navigate to the root directory of your project (where your `package.json` file is located), and run the following command:

```
npm install mongoose
```

This command will download and install the Mongoose package and its dependencies.

Connecting to MongoDB

Once Mongoose is installed, we can establish a connection to our MongoDB database. Let's create a new file named db.js inside our "server" folder. This file will handle the database connection logic.

Open db.js in your code editor and add the following code:

```
const mongoose = require('mongoose');


const connectDB = async () => {

  try {

    await
mongoose.connect('mongodb://localhost:27017/
mymern', {

      useNewUrlParser: true,

      useUnifiedTopology: true,

    });
```

```
    console.log('Connected to MongoDB');

  } catch (error) {

    console.error('Failed to connect to
MongoDB:', error);

    process.exit(1); // Exit process with
failure

  }

};



module.exports = connectDB;
```

In this code:

- We first require the mongoose module.

- We define an asynchronous function connectDB that handles the database connection logic.

- Inside connectDB, we use mongoose.connect() to establish a connection to our MongoDB database. We provide the connection string, which specifies the database host (localhost), port (27017), and database name (mymern). You can replace mymern with the name of your database.

- We also pass some options to mongoose.connect() to ensure a stable connection.

- If the connection is successful, we log a message to the console.

- If there's an error during the connection process, we catch it, log an error message, and exit the process with a failure code.

- Finally, we export the `connectDB` function so that we can use it in other parts of our application.

Defining a Schema

Now that we've established a connection to our database, let's define a schema for our data. Suppose we want to store information about users in our database. Each user will have a name, email address, and password.

Let's create a new file named `User.js` inside a "models" folder within our "server" directory. This file will contain the schema definition for our User model.

Open `User.js` and add the following code:

```
const mongoose = require('mongoose');



const UserSchema = new mongoose.Schema({

  name: {

    type: String,

    required: true,

  },
```

```
email: {

  type: String,

  required: true,

  unique: true,

},

password: {

  type: String,

  required: true,

},

});


module.exports = mongoose.model('User',
UserSchema);
```

In this code:

- We require the mongoose module.

- We create a new schema using mongoose.Schema().

- We define the fields for our User schema: name, email, and password.

- For each field, we specify its data type (e.g., `String`) and any validation rules (e.g., `required: true, unique: true`).

- Finally, we create a model named `User` using `mongoose.model()`. This model will be used to interact with the "users" collection in our database.

Creating a User

Now that we have our User model defined, let's create a new user. We can do this using the `create()` method of our User model.

Open your `index.js` file (the main server file) and add the following code after requiring the `express` module:

```
const express = require('express');

const connectDB = require('./db');

const User = require('./models/User');


// ... (rest of the code)


connectDB(); // Connect to MongoDB


// ... (rest of the code)


app.post('/users', async (req, res) => {
```

45

```
try {

  const newUser = new User({

    name: req.body.name,

    email: req.body.email,

    password: req.body.password,

  });


  const user = await newUser.save();


  res.json(user);

} catch (error) {

  console.error('Error creating user:',
error);

  res.status(500).send('Server Error');

}

});


// ... (rest of the code)
```

In this code:

- We call `connectDB()` to establish a connection to our database.

- We define a route for POST requests to `/users`.

- Inside the route handler, we create a new instance of the `User` model using the data received in the request body.

- We save the new user to the database using `newUser.save()`. This method returns a promise that resolves with the saved user document.

- We send the saved user document as a JSON response to the client.

- If there's an error during the process, we catch it, log an error message, and send a 500 (Internal Server Error) response to the client.

Retrieving Users

Let's add a route to retrieve all users from the database. We can do this using the `find()` method of our User model.

Add the following code to your `index.js` file:

```
// ... (rest of the code)


app.get('/users', async (req, res) => {

  try {

    const users = await User.find();
```

```
    res.json(users);

  } catch (error) {

    console.error('Error retrieving users:',
error);

    res.status(500).send('Server Error');

  }

});


// ... (rest of the code)
```

In this code:

- We define a route for GET requests to /users.

- Inside the route handler, we use User.find() to retrieve all users from the database. This method returns a promise that resolves with an array of user documents.

- We send the array of users as a JSON response to the client.

- If there's an error during the process, we catch it, log an error message, and send a 500 response to the client.

Retrieving a Single User

We can also retrieve a specific user from the database based on their ID. We can do this using the `findById()` method of our User model.

Add the following code to your `index.js` file:

```
// ... (rest of the code)


app.get('/users/:id', async (req, res) => {

    try {

        const user = await
User.findById(req.params.id);


        if (!user) {

            return res.status(404).json({ msg:
'User not found' });

        }


        res.json(user);

    } catch (error) {

        console.error('Error retrieving user:',
error);

        res.status(500).send('Server Error');
```

```
    }

});
```

```
// ... (rest of the code)
```

In this code:

- We define a route for GET requests to `/users/:id`. The `:id` part indicates a dynamic route parameter that will capture the user's ID.

- Inside the route handler, we use `User.findById()` to retrieve the user with the specified ID.

- If the user is not found, we send a 404 (Not Found) response to the client.

- If the user is found, we send the user document as a JSON response to the client.

- If there's an error during the process, we catch it, log an error message, and send a 500 response to the client.

Updating a User

Let's add a route to update an existing user's information. We can do this using the `findByIdAndUpdate()` method of our User model.

Add the following code to your `index.js` file:

```
// ... (rest of the code)


app.put('/users/:id', async (req, res) => {

  try {

    const user = await
User.findByIdAndUpdate(

      req.params.id,

      {

        $set: req.body, // Update the user's
fields with the request body data

      },

      { new: true } // Return the updated
user document

    );


    if (!user) {

      return res.status(404).json({ msg:
'User not found' });

    }


    res.json(user);

  } catch (error) {
```

```
    console.error('Error updating user:',
error);

    res.status(500).send('Server Error');

  }

});



// ... (rest of the code)
```

In this code:

- We define a route for PUT requests to `/users/:id`.

- Inside the route handler, we use
  `User.findByIdAndUpdate()` to find the user with
  the specified ID and update their fields with the data
  received in the request body.

- We use the `$set` operator to update the user's fields.

- We pass the `{ new: true }` option to
  `findByIdAndUpdate()` to ensure that the updated user
  document is returned.

- If the user is not found, we send a 404 response to the
  client.

- If the user is found and updated, we send the updated user
  document as a JSON response to the client.

- If there's an error during the process, we catch it, log an error message, and send a 500 response to the client.

Deleting a User

Finally, let's add a route to delete a user from the database. We can do this using the findByIdAndRemove() method of our User model.

Add the following code to your index.js file:

```
// ... (rest of the code)



app.delete('/users/:id', async (req, res) =>
{

   try {

      const user = await
User.findByIdAndRemove(req.params.id);



      if (!user) {

         return res.status(404).json({ msg:
'User not found' });

      }



      res.json({ msg: 'User removed' });

   } catch (error) {
```

```
    console.error('Error deleting user:',
error);

    res.status(500).send('Server Error');

  }

});



// ... (rest of the code)
```

In this code:

- We define a route for DELETE requests to /users/:id.

- Inside the route handler, we use
  User.findByIdAndRemove() to find the user with
  the specified ID and remove them from the database.

- If the user is not found, we send a 404 response to the
  client.

- If the user is found and removed, we send a JSON response
  indicating that the user was removed.

- If there's an error during the process, we catch it, log an
  error message, and send a 500 response to the client.

Now you have a basic understanding of how MongoDB and
Mongoose work together in a MERN stack application, providing
the "M" that underpins your data management. You've learned
how to connect to your database, define schemas, and perform
CRUD (Create, Read, Update, Delete) operations on your data

using Mongoose models. This sets the stage for building more complex and feature-rich applications that rely on persistent data storage. As you progress through this book, you'll encounter more advanced Mongoose features and techniques that will empower you to build robust and scalable back-end systems.

Chapter Six: Creating a RESTful API with Express and MongoDB

In the previous chapter, we delved into the world of MongoDB and Mongoose, learning how to connect to our database, define schemas, and perform CRUD operations on our data. Now, it's time to bridge the gap between our back-end and front-end by creating a RESTful API using Express.js and MongoDB. This API will serve as the communication channel, allowing our front-end React application to interact with the data stored in our database.

What is a RESTful API?

Before we dive into building our API, let's clarify what a RESTful API is. REST stands for Representational State Transfer, and it's an architectural style for designing networked applications. A RESTful API adheres to the principles of REST, providing a standardized way for different systems to communicate with each other over the internet.

Think of a RESTful API as a waiter in a restaurant. The waiter takes your order (request), communicates it to the kitchen (back-end), and brings you the food (response). The waiter follows a set of rules and conventions to ensure that the order is communicated accurately and efficiently.

RESTful APIs use HTTP methods (GET, POST, PUT, DELETE) to perform actions on resources. Resources are the entities that your API exposes, such as users, products, or articles. Each resource has a unique URL (Uniform Resource Locator) that identifies it.

For example, if our API exposes users as a resource, we might have the following URLs:

- `GET /users`: Retrieve a list of all users

- `GET /users/:id`: Retrieve a specific user by ID

- `POST /users`: Create a new user

- `PUT /users/:id`: Update an existing user by ID

- `DELETE /users/:id`: Delete a user by ID

RESTful APIs typically use JSON (JavaScript Object Notation) as the data format for communication. JSON is a lightweight and human-readable format that's well-suited for representing data structures.

Designing Our API Endpoints

Let's design the endpoints for our API. We'll continue with the example of managing users, but you can adapt these principles to any resource you want to expose through your API.

We'll define the following endpoints:

Method	Endpoint	Description
GET	/api/users	Retrieve all users
GET	/api/users/:id	Retrieve a specific user by ID
POST	/api/users	Create a new user
PUT	/api/users/:id	Update an existing user by ID
DELETE	/api/users/:id	Delete a user by ID

We'll prefix our endpoints with `/api` to distinguish them from other routes in our application.

Implementing the API Endpoints

Now, let's implement these endpoints in our Express.js application. We'll build upon the code we wrote in the previous chapter, where we defined our User model and established a connection to our MongoDB database.

Open your `index.js` file and add the following code after the existing routes:

```javascript
// ... (existing code)

// User API endpoints
app.get('/api/users', async (req, res) => {
  try {
    const users = await User.find();
    res.json(users);
  } catch (error) {
    console.error('Error retrieving users:', error);
    res.status(500).send('Server Error');
  }
});

app.get('/api/users/:id', async (req, res) => {
  try {
    const user = await User.findById(req.params.id);
```

```
    if (!user) {

        return res.status(404).json({ msg:
'User not found' });

    }

    res.json(user);

  } catch (error) {

    console.error('Error retrieving user:',
error);

    res.status(500).send('Server Error');

  }

});


app.post('/api/users', async (req, res) => {

  try {

    const newUser = new User({

      name: req.body.name,

      email: req.body.email,

      password: req.body.password,

    });

    const user = await newUser.save();
```

```
    res.json(user);

  } catch (error) {

    console.error('Error creating user:',
error);

    res.status(500).send('Server Error');

  }

});


app.put('/api/users/:id', async (req, res)
=> {

  try {

    const user = await
User.findByIdAndUpdate(

      req.params.id,

      { $set: req.body },

      { new: true }

    );

    if (!user) {

      return res.status(404).json({ msg:
'User not found' });

    }

    res.json(user);
```

```
  } catch (error) {

    console.error('Error updating user:',
error);

    res.status(500).send('Server Error');

  }

});


app.delete('/api/users/:id', async (req,
res) => {

  try {

    const user = await
User.findByIdAndRemove(req.params.id);

    if (!user) {

      return res.status(404).json({ msg:
'User not found' });

    }

    res.json({ msg: 'User removed' });

  } catch (error) {

    console.error('Error deleting user:',
error);

    res.status(500).send('Server Error');

  }
```

```
});
```

```
// ... (rest of the code)
```

In this code, we've defined the five API endpoints we outlined earlier. Each endpoint corresponds to a specific HTTP method and URL. Inside each endpoint handler, we use Mongoose methods to interact with our MongoDB database.

For example, in the `GET /api/users` endpoint, we use `User.find()` to retrieve all users from the database and send them as a JSON response. In the `POST /api/users` endpoint, we create a new user document using the data received in the request body and save it to the database.

Testing the API

Now that we've implemented our API endpoints, let's test them out. We can use tools like Postman or Insomnia to send HTTP requests to our API and inspect the responses.

For example, to test the `GET /api/users` endpoint, you would send a GET request to `http://localhost:5000/api/users` using Postman or Insomnia. The response should be a JSON array containing all the users in our database.

Similarly, you can test the other endpoints by sending requests with the appropriate HTTP method and data.

Error Handling and Validation

In a real-world application, it's crucial to handle errors gracefully and validate the data received from the client. We can add error handling and validation logic to our API endpoints to ensure that our application behaves predictably and provides informative error messages.

For example, in the POST /api/users endpoint, we can validate the request body to ensure that the required fields (name, email, password) are present and meet certain criteria (e.g., email format). We can also handle errors that might occur during the database interaction, such as duplicate email addresses.

Here's an example of how we can add validation to the POST /api/users endpoint:

```
app.post('/api/users', async (req, res) => {

  const { name, email, password } =
req.body;


  // Validation

  if (!name || !email || !password) {

    return res.status(400).json({ msg:
'Please enter all fields' });

  }


  if (!isValidEmail(email)) {

    return res.status(400).json({ msg:
'Please enter a valid email' });
```

```
  }


  // ... (rest of the code)

});



// Helper function to validate email format

function isValidEmail(email) {

  // Regular expression for email validation

  const emailRegex =
/^[^\s@]+@[^\s@]+\.[^\s@]+$/;

  return emailRegex.test(email);

}
```

In this code, we've added validation logic to check if the required fields are present and if the email format is valid. If the validation fails, we send a 400 (Bad Request) response to the client with an informative error message.

Securing Your API

Security is paramount when building APIs. You need to protect your API from unauthorized access and ensure that sensitive data is transmitted securely.

There are various techniques for securing APIs, including:

- **Authentication:** Verify the identity of the client making the request.

- **Authorization:** Determine if the client has permission to access the requested resource.

- **Input validation:** Prevent malicious input from affecting your application.

- **Rate limiting:** Prevent abuse by limiting the number of requests a client can make within a given time frame.

- **HTTPS:** Encrypt communication between the client and the server.

We'll explore these security concepts in more detail in later chapters.

Documenting Your API

Documentation is essential for making your API easy to understand and use. API documentation provides developers with information about the available endpoints, their parameters, the expected responses, and any authentication or authorization requirements.

There are various tools and formats for documenting APIs, including:

- **Swagger/OpenAPI:** A specification and tools for describing RESTful APIs.

- **Postman:** A tool for testing and documenting APIs.

- **API Blueprint:** A Markdown-based language for describing APIs.

Choose a documentation format that suits your needs and ensure that your API documentation is up-to-date and accurate.

By mastering the art of creating RESTful APIs with Express and MongoDB, you unlock the ability to build powerful and scalable back-end systems that seamlessly integrate with your front-end applications. As you progress through this book, you'll encounter more advanced API design patterns and techniques that will further enhance your back-end development skills. Remember, a well-designed and well-documented API is the cornerstone of a successful MERN stack application, enabling smooth communication and data exchange between the front-end and back-end components.

Chapter Seven: Introduction to React.js

Having established a robust back-end with Node.js, Express.js, and MongoDB, it's time to shift our focus to the front-end, the part of our application that users directly interact with. In this chapter, we'll introduce React.js, a powerful JavaScript library that has revolutionized the way we build user interfaces. We'll explore its core concepts, understand its component-based architecture, and lay the groundwork for crafting dynamic and engaging user experiences.

React.js: A JavaScript Library for Building User Interfaces

React.js, often referred to as simply React, is a JavaScript library developed and maintained by Facebook. It's designed specifically for building user interfaces (UIs), the visual part of web applications that users see and interact with. React has gained immense popularity in recent years, becoming one of the most widely used front-end libraries in the web development landscape.

React's popularity stems from several key factors:

- **Component-Based Architecture:** React promotes a component-based approach, where you build your UI by creating reusable components, each responsible for a specific part of the interface. This modularity makes your code more organized, easier to maintain, and promotes code reusability.

- **Declarative Programming:** React embraces a declarative style of programming, where you describe what you want your UI to look like, and React takes care of updating the UI based on changes in data or user interactions. This contrasts with imperative programming, where you explicitly specify how the UI should be updated, often leading to more complex and error-prone code.

- **Virtual DOM:** React utilizes a Virtual DOM, a lightweight representation of the actual DOM (Document Object Model). When changes occur in your application's data or state, React updates the Virtual DOM first and then efficiently compares it with the actual DOM, applying only the necessary changes to the browser's DOM. This approach minimizes direct manipulation of the DOM, resulting in faster updates and improved performance.

- **JSX:** React introduces JSX (JavaScript XML), a syntax extension that allows you to write HTML-like code within your JavaScript. JSX makes it more intuitive to describe the structure and appearance of your UI components, blurring the lines between HTML and JavaScript.

- **Large and Active Community:** React boasts a vast and active community of developers, contributing to its growth, providing support, and creating a wealth of resources, tutorials, and libraries. This vibrant ecosystem makes it easier to learn React and find solutions to common challenges.

Understanding the DOM and Virtual DOM

Before we delve deeper into React's component-based architecture, let's briefly discuss the DOM and React's Virtual DOM.

The DOM (Document Object Model) is a tree-like representation of a web page's structure. It's created by the browser when it parses HTML and provides a way for JavaScript to interact with and manipulate the elements on the page.

However, direct manipulation of the DOM can be expensive in terms of performance, especially when dealing with frequent updates. Each time you change an element in the DOM, the browser needs to repaint and reflow the page, which can be time-consuming.

React addresses this performance bottleneck by introducing the Virtual DOM. The Virtual DOM is a lightweight copy of the actual DOM that React maintains in memory. When changes occur in your application's data or state, React updates the Virtual DOM first.

Then, React performs a "diffing" algorithm to compare the Virtual DOM with the previous version of the Virtual DOM. It identifies the minimal set of changes that need to be applied to the actual DOM to reflect the updated state.

Finally, React efficiently applies these changes to the actual DOM, minimizing the number of browser repaints and reflows, resulting in faster updates and improved performance.

Components: The Building Blocks of React Applications

React applications are built using components. Components are reusable UI elements that encapsulate a specific part of the interface, along with its logic and appearance. Think of components as Lego blocks – you can combine and reuse them to create complex and dynamic UIs.

React components can be either functional components or class components. Functional components are simpler and more concise, typically used for presentational purposes, while class components offer more features and are suitable for managing state and complex logic.

Let's illustrate the concept of components with a simple example. Suppose we want to create a component that displays a greeting message. We can define a functional component like this:

```
function Greeting(props) {

  return (
```

```
<div>

    Hello, {props.name}!

</div>

  );

}
```

In this code:

- We define a functional component named Greeting.

- The component takes an object called props (short for properties) as an argument. Props are used to pass data to components.

- Inside the component, we return JSX code that describes the structure and appearance of the component. In this case, we return a div element that contains the greeting message.

- We use curly braces { } within the JSX to embed JavaScript expressions. In this case, we embed the props.name value to display the name passed to the component.

To use this component, we can simply render it within another component or within the root of our React application:

```
function App() {
```

```
    return (

      <div>

        <Greeting name="John" />

        <Greeting name="Jane" />

      </div>

    );

}
```

In this code:

- We define another functional component named App.

- Inside the App component, we render two instances of the Greeting component, passing different names as props.

When this code is rendered, it will display the following output in the browser:

```
Hello, John!

Hello, Jane!
```

This simple example demonstrates the basic concept of React components and how they can be used to build modular and reusable UI elements.

Props: Passing Data to Components

As we saw in the previous example, props are used to pass data to components. Props are read-only, meaning that a component cannot modify its own props.

Props can be of any data type, including strings, numbers, booleans, objects, and arrays. You can pass props to a component when you render it, as we did in the `App` component example.

Inside the component, you can access the props using the `props` object. For example, to access the `name` prop, you would use `props.name`.

State: Managing Component-Specific Data

While props are used to pass data from parent components to child components, state is used to manage data that's specific to a component. State represents the internal data of a component that can change over time, such as user input, loading status, or the visibility of elements.

In functional components, you can manage state using the `useState` hook. In class components, you manage state using the `this.state` object.

Let's illustrate the concept of state with an example. Suppose we want to create a counter component that allows the user to increment and decrement a counter value. We can define a functional component like this:

```
import React, { useState } from 'react';



function Counter() {
```

```
const [count, setCount] = useState(0);


const increment = () => {

  setCount(count + 1);

};


const decrement = () => {

  setCount(count - 1);

};


return (

  <div>

    <p>Count: {count}</p>

    <button
onClick={increment}>Increment</button>

    <button
onClick={decrement}>Decrement</button>

  </div>

);

}
```

```
export default Counter;
```

In this code:

- We import the `useState` hook from React.

- We initialize the `count` state variable to 0 using `useState(0)`. `useState` returns an array containing the current state value and a function to update the state.

- We define two functions, `increment` and `decrement`, that update the `count` state using `setCount`.

- We render the `count` value and two buttons that call the `increment` and `decrement` functions when clicked.

When this component is rendered, it will display the counter value and two buttons. Clicking the "Increment" button will increase the counter value, and clicking the "Decrement" button will decrease it.

Lifecycle Methods in Class Components

In class components, you have access to lifecycle methods that allow you to control the behavior of your component at different stages of its lifecycle. These methods are called automatically by React at specific points in a component's existence.

Some common lifecycle methods include:

- `componentDidMount()`: Called after the component has been rendered to the DOM.

- `componentDidUpdate()`: Called after the component has been updated.

- `componentWillUnmount()`: Called before the component is removed from the DOM.

You can use these lifecycle methods to perform actions such as fetching data from an API, subscribing to events, or cleaning up resources when the component is unmounted.

Event Handling in React

React provides a way to handle events, such as user clicks, mouseovers, and form submissions, using event handlers. Event handlers are functions that are executed when a specific event occurs on an element.

In React, you typically attach event handlers to elements using JSX attributes. For example, to handle a click event on a button, you would use the `onClick` attribute:

```
<button onClick={handleClick}>Click me</button>
```

In this code, `handleClick` is the event handler function that will be executed when the button is clicked.

Conditional Rendering

React allows you to conditionally render elements based on certain conditions. This means that you can show or hide elements depending on the state of your application or user interactions.

You can achieve conditional rendering using JavaScript's `if` statements, ternary operators, or logical AND operators within your JSX.

For example, suppose we want to display a message only if a user is logged in. We can use a ternary operator to conditionally render the message:

```
function App() {

  const isLoggedIn = true;


  return (

    <div>

      {isLoggedIn ? <p>Welcome, user!</p> :
null}

    </div>

  );

}
```

In this code, if isLoggedIn is true, the p element containing the welcome message will be rendered. Otherwise, nothing will be rendered in its place.

Lists and Keys

React provides a convenient way to render lists of items using the map() method. The map() method iterates over an array and returns a new array where each element is transformed based on the provided function.

When rendering lists in React, it's important to provide a unique key prop for each item in the list. The key prop helps React identify which items have changed, been added, or removed, allowing it to efficiently update the UI.

Here's an example of how to render a list of items in React:

```
function App() {

  const items = ['Item 1', 'Item 2', 'Item
3'];


  return (

    <ul>

      {items.map((item, index) => (

        <li key={index}>{item}</li>

      ))}

    </ul>

  );

}
```

In this code, we use the map() method to iterate over the items array and render a li element for each item. We provide the index as the key prop for each item.

Forms in React

React provides a way to handle forms and user input. You can create forms using standard HTML form elements, such as `input`, `textarea`, and `select`.

To handle form submissions, you typically attach an `onSubmit` event handler to the form element. Inside the event handler, you can access the form data and perform actions such as sending the data to an API or updating the component's state.

Working with APIs in React

React applications often need to interact with APIs to fetch or send data. You can use libraries like `fetch` or `axios` to make HTTP requests to APIs from your React components.

Styling React Applications

There are various ways to style React applications, including:

- **Inline styles:** You can apply styles directly to elements using the `style` attribute.

- **CSS Modules:** You can create modular CSS files that are scoped to specific components.

- **Styled Components:** You can use a library like Styled Components to write CSS-in-JS.

React Developer Tools

The React Developer Tools are a browser extension that provides helpful tools for debugging and inspecting React applications. You can use the React Developer Tools to view the component tree, inspect component props and state, and track performance.

Conclusion

React.js has emerged as a dominant force in front-end development, empowering developers to build dynamic, interactive, and performant user interfaces. Its component-based architecture, declarative programming model, and efficient Virtual DOM make it a compelling choice for crafting modern web applications. As you continue your journey through this book, you'll delve deeper into React's intricacies, mastering its features and building increasingly complex and engaging user interfaces. With React as your front-end arsenal, you'll be well-equipped to create captivating web experiences that delight users and elevate your MERN stack applications to new heights.

Chapter Eight: Understanding JSX and React Components

In the previous chapter, we took our first steps into the world of React.js, exploring its core concepts, component-based architecture, and the power of declarative programming. Now, it's time to delve deeper into the heart of React development: JSX and React components. We'll unravel the mysteries of JSX syntax, learn how to create and compose components, and discover the elegance of building user interfaces with React's building blocks.

JSX: A Bridge Between HTML and JavaScript

JSX, which stands for JavaScript XML, is a syntax extension that allows you to write HTML-like code within your JavaScript. It might seem a bit unusual at first, but JSX plays a crucial role in React development, making it more intuitive and efficient to describe the structure and appearance of your UI components.

Think of JSX as a translator that bridges the gap between HTML and JavaScript. It allows you to express your UI's structure using familiar HTML-like syntax while seamlessly integrating it with JavaScript's logic and data.

Let's illustrate the power of JSX with a simple example. Suppose we want to create a component that displays a heading and a paragraph. We can do this using JSX like this:

```
function MyComponent() {

return (

<div>

  <h1>Hello, React!</h1>

  <p>This is a paragraph.</p>
```

```
</div>

);

}
```

In this code:

- We define a functional component named `MyComponent`.

- Inside the component, we return JSX code that represents the structure of our UI.

- We use HTML-like tags, such as `<h1>`, `<p>`, and `<div>`, to describe the elements we want to render.

- The JSX code is enclosed within parentheses `()` to indicate that it's a JavaScript expression.

When React encounters JSX code, it transforms it into regular JavaScript code that the browser can understand and execute. For instance, the JSX code above would be transformed into something like this:

function MyComponent() {

return React.createElement(

```
'div',
```

```
null,
```

```
React.createElement('h1', null, 'Hello,
React!'),
```

```
React.createElement('p', null, 'This is a
paragraph.')
```

);

}

As you can see, the JSX code is translated into nested calls to `React.createElement()`, which is React's way of creating and managing UI elements.

Embedding JavaScript Expressions in JSX

JSX's power goes beyond simply writing HTML-like code within JavaScript. It also allows you to embed JavaScript expressions within your JSX, making it dynamic and data-driven.

You can embed JavaScript expressions within JSX by enclosing them in curly braces { }. For example, suppose we want to display a variable's value within our JSX. We can do this like this:

```
function MyComponent() {

const name = 'John';

return (

<div>

  <h1>Hello, {name}!</h1>

</div>

);

}
```

In this code:

- We define a variable named `name` and assign it the value 'John'.

- Inside the JSX, we embed the `name` variable within curly braces { }.

When this code is rendered, React will evaluate the JavaScript expression `name` and replace it with its value, resulting in the following output:

Hello, John!

You can embed any valid JavaScript expression within JSX, including function calls, arithmetic operations, and conditional expressions.

JSX Attributes

Just like HTML elements, JSX elements can have attributes. Attributes provide additional information about the element, such as its class, id, or style.

In JSX, you specify attributes using camelCase naming convention. For example, to add a class attribute to a `div` element, you would use `className` instead of `class`:

{/* Content */}

Similarly, to add an id attribute, you would use `id`:

{/* Content */}

You can also specify inline styles using the `style` attribute. The `style` attribute takes an object where the keys are CSS property names in camelCase and the values are CSS property values:

{/* Content */}

JSX Event Handling

JSX allows you to attach event handlers to elements, just like you would in regular HTML. Event handlers are functions that are executed when a specific event occurs on an element, such as a click, mouseover, or form submission.

In JSX, you attach event handlers using camelCase naming convention. For example, to attach a click event handler to a button, you would use `onClick`:

function MyComponent() {

const handleClick = () => {

```
console.log('Button clicked!');
```

};

return (

```
<button onClick={handleClick}>Click
me</button>
```

);

}

In this code:

- We define a function named `handleClick` that will be executed when the button is clicked.

- We attach the `handleClick` function to the button's `onClick` attribute.

When the button is clicked, the `handleClick` function will be executed, logging the message "Button clicked!" to the console.

React Components: Building Blocks of User Interfaces

React applications are built using components. Components are reusable UI elements that encapsulate a specific part of the interface, along with its logic and appearance. Think of components as Lego blocks – you can combine and reuse them to create complex and dynamic UIs.

React components can be either functional components or class components. Functional components are simpler and more concise, typically used for presentational purposes, while class components offer more features and are suitable for managing state and complex logic.

Let's explore both types of components in more detail.

Functional Components

Functional components are the simplest type of React component. They are essentially JavaScript functions that accept props as input and return JSX that describes the component's UI.

Here's an example of a functional component that displays a greeting message:

```
function Greeting(props) {

return (

<div>

  Hello, {props.name}!

</div>

);

}
```

In this code:

- We define a functional component named Greeting.

- The component takes an object called props as an argument. Props are used to pass data to components.

- Inside the component, we return JSX code that describes the structure and appearance of the component. In this case, we return a `div` element that contains the greeting message.

- We use curly braces { } within the JSX to embed the `props.name` value to display the name passed to the component.

To use this component, we can simply render it within another component or within the root of our React application:

```
function App() {

return (

<div>

  <Greeting name="John" />

  <Greeting name="Jane" />

</div>

);

}
```

In this code:

- We define another functional component named `App`.

- Inside the `App` component, we render two instances of the `Greeting` component, passing different names as props.

When this code is rendered, it will display the following output in the browser:

Hello, John!

Hello, Jane!

Class Components

Class components are more complex than functional components, but they offer more features, such as state management and lifecycle methods.

Here's an example of a class component that manages a counter:

import React from 'react';

class Counter extends React.Component {

constructor(props) {

```
super(props);
```

```
this.state = { count: 0 };
```

}

increment = () => {

```
this.setState({ count: this.state.count + 1
});
```

};

decrement = () => {

```
this.setState({ count: this.state.count - 1
});
```

};

render() {

```
return (
```

```
<div>

    <p>Count: {this.state.count}</p>

    <button
onClick={this.increment}>Increment</button>

    <button
onClick={this.decrement}>Decrement</button>

</div>

);

}

}
```

export default Counter;

In this code:

- We define a class component named `Counter` that extends `React.Component`.

- In the constructor, we initialize the component's state using `this.state`.

- We define two methods, `increment` and `decrement`, that update the component's state using `this.setState`.

- In the `render` method, we return JSX that describes the component's UI. We access the component's state using `this.state`.

When this component is rendered, it will display the counter value and two buttons. Clicking the "Increment" button will increase the counter value, and clicking the "Decrement" button will decrease it.

Component Composition: Building Complex UIs

One of the key benefits of React's component-based architecture is the ability to compose components, meaning you can build complex UIs by combining smaller, reusable components.

For example, suppose we want to create a component that displays a list of users. We can create a separate component for each user and then compose them within a parent component to create the user list.

Here's an example:

function User(props) {

return (

```
<li>
```

```
  {props.name}  ({props.email})
```

```
</li>
```

);

}

function UserList(props) {

return (

```
<ul>
```

```
  {props.users.map((user) => (
```

```
    <User key={user.id} name={user.name}
email={user.email} />
```

```
        ) ) }

</ul>

);

}

function App() {

const users = [

{ id: 1, name: 'John', email:
'john@example.com' },

{ id: 2, name: 'Jane', email:
'jane@example.com' },

];

return (

<div>

   <UserList users={users} />

</div>

);

}
```

In this code:

- We define a `User` component that displays a single user's name and email.

- We define a `UserList` component that takes an array of users as props and renders a list of `User` components.

- We define an `App` component that renders the `UserList` component with a sample array of users.

When this code is rendered, it will display a list of users in the browser.

Props Validation: Ensuring Data Integrity

Props validation is a technique used to ensure that the data passed to a component through props is of the expected type and format. This helps prevent errors and makes your components more robust.

You can perform props validation using the `prop-types` library. The `prop-types` library provides a set of validators that you can use to specify the expected type and format of your component's props.

Here's an example of how to use `prop-types` to validate the props of the `User` component:

import PropTypes from 'prop-types';

function User(props) {

return (

<li>

  {props.name} ({props.email})

</li>

);

}

User.propTypes = {

name: PropTypes.string.isRequired,

91

email: PropTypes.string.isRequired,

};

In this code:

- We import the `PropTypes` object from the `prop-types` library.

- We define the `propTypes` property on the `User` component.

- We specify that the `name` and `email` props are required and must be strings.

If you try to render the `User` component with invalid props, you'll see a warning in the console.

Default Props: Providing Fallback Values

Default props allow you to provide fallback values for props that are not explicitly passed to a component. This can be useful for making your components more flexible and resilient to missing props.

You can specify default props using the `defaultProps` property on a component.

Here's an example of how to specify default props for the `User` component:

```
function User(props) {

return (

<li>

   {props.name} ({props.email})
```

```
</li>

);

}
```

User.defaultProps = {

name: 'Anonymous',

email: 'anonymous@example.com',

};

In this code:

- We define the `defaultProps` property on the `User` component.

- We specify that the default value for the `name` prop is 'Anonymous' and the default value for the `email` prop is 'anonymous@example.com'.

If you render the `User` component without explicitly passing the `name` or `email` props, it will use the default values instead.

By mastering JSX and React components, you gain a deep understanding of the core building blocks that empower you to craft dynamic and interactive user interfaces. JSX's elegance allows you to seamlessly blend HTML-like syntax with JavaScript's logic, while React's component model promotes reusability, modularity, and maintainability. As you progress through this book, you'll encounter more advanced component patterns and techniques that will further enhance your React development skills. With JSX and React components as your foundation, you'll be well-equipped to build captivating web experiences that delight users and elevate your MERN stack applications to new heights.

Chapter Nine: Building Your First React Application

In the previous chapter, we explored the intricacies of JSX and React components, gaining a deeper understanding of how React's building blocks work together to create dynamic and interactive user interfaces. Now, it's time to put this knowledge into practice and build our first React application. We'll guide you through the process of setting up a new React project, creating components, managing state, and handling events, culminating in a simple yet functional application that showcases the power of React.

Creating a New React Project

Before we can start building our application, we need to set up a new React project. The easiest way to do this is by using Create React App, a command-line tool that generates a basic React project structure with all the necessary configurations.

Open your terminal or command prompt and navigate to the directory where you want to create your project. Then, run the following command:

```
npx create-react-app my-react-app
```

Replace `my-react-app` with the desired name for your project. This command will create a new directory named `my-react-app` and install all the necessary dependencies for a React project.

Once the installation is complete, navigate to the project directory:

```
cd my-react-app
```

You can now start the development server by running:

```
npm start
```

This command will launch the development server and open your application in a new browser window. You should see a basic React welcome page.

Exploring the Project Structure

Let's take a moment to explore the project structure that Create React App has generated for us. Open the my-react-app directory in your code editor. You'll see several files and folders:

- public: This folder contains static assets, such as the index.html file, which serves as the entry point for our application.

- src: This folder contains the source code for our React application.

- App.js: This is the main component of our application. It's the component that's rendered at the root of our application.

- index.js: This file is responsible for rendering the App component into the root element in the index.html file.

- `App.css`: This file contains the CSS styles for the `App` component.

- `index.css`: This file contains global CSS styles that apply to the entire application.

- `package.json`: This file contains metadata about our project, including its name, version, dependencies, and scripts.

Building a Simple Counter Application

Let's build a simple counter application to demonstrate the fundamental concepts of React development. Our application will display a counter value and two buttons: one to increment the counter and one to decrement it.

Open the `App.js` file in your code editor and replace its contents with the following code:

```
import React, { useState } from 'react';

import './App.css';


function App() {

  const [count, setCount] = useState(0);


  const increment = () => {

    setCount(count + 1);

  };
```

```
const decrement = () => {

  setCount(count - 1);

};


return (
```

Counter

```
Count: {count}

        Increment

        Decrement



    );

}



export default App;
```

In this code:

- We import the `useState` hook from React. This hook allows us to manage the state of our component.

- We initialize the `count` state variable to 0 using `useState(0)`. `useState` returns an array containing the current state value and a function to update the state.

- We define two functions, `increment` and `decrement`, that update the `count` state using `setCount`.

- We render the `count` value and two buttons that call the `increment` and `decrement` functions when clicked.

Save the file and observe the changes in your browser. You should now see a counter application with a counter value of 0 and two buttons. Clicking the "Increment" button will increase the counter value, and clicking the "Decrement" button will decrease it.

Creating a Separate Counter Component

To demonstrate component composition, let's create a separate component for the counter logic and UI. Create a new file named `Counter.js` in the `src` folder and add the following code:

```
import React, { useState } from 'react';



function Counter() {

  const [count, setCount] = useState(0);



  const increment = () => {

    setCount(count + 1);

  };
```

```
  const decrement = () => {

    setCount(count - 1);

  };


  return (




Count: {count}


      Increment

      Decrement




  );

}


export default Counter;
```

This code is essentially the same as the code we had in `App.js`, but now it's encapsulated within a separate component named `Counter`.

Now, let's import and use this `Counter` component in our `App.js` file:

```
import React from 'react';

import './App.css';

import Counter from './Counter';


function App() {

    return (
```

Counter Application

```
  );

}



export default App;
```

In this code:

- We import the `Counter` component from `./Counter`.

- We render the `Counter` component within the `App` component.

Save the files and observe the changes in your browser. You should still see the same counter application, but now the counter logic and UI are managed by a separate component.

Passing Props to the Counter Component

Let's make our `Counter` component more flexible by allowing the initial counter value to be passed as a prop. Modify the `Counter` component code as follows:

```
import React, { useState } from 'react';


function Counter(props) {

  const [count, setCount] =
useState(props.initialValue || 0);


  // ... (rest of the code)

}


export default Counter;
```

In this code:

- We access the `initialValue` prop using `props.initialValue`.

- We use the `initialValue` prop as the initial value for the `count` state variable. If the `initialValue` prop is not provided, we default to 0.

Now, let's pass an initial value to the `Counter` component from the `App` component:

```
import React from 'react';

import './App.css';

import Counter from './Counter';


function App() {

  return (
```

Counter Application

```
    );

}


export default Counter;
```

In this code:

- We pass the value 10 as the `initialValue` prop to the `Counter` component.

Save the files and observe the changes in your browser. The counter should now start at 10 instead of 0.

Styling the Counter Application

Let's add some basic styling to our counter application. Open the `App.css` file and add the following CSS rules:

```css
.App {

  text-align: center;

}


.App h1 {

  margin-bottom: 20px;

}


.App button {

  margin: 0 10px;

  padding: 10px 20px;

  font-size: 16px;

  border: none;

  border-radius: 5px;

  background-color: #007bff;

  color: #fff;

  cursor: pointer;

}
```

These CSS rules will center the content, add some margin to the heading, and style the buttons.

Save the file and observe the changes in your browser. The counter application should now have a more visually appealing appearance.

Handling Events in the Counter Component

Let's add some event handling to our counter application. We'll add a feature that displays an alert message when the counter value reaches a certain threshold.

Modify the Counter component code as follows:

```
import React, { useState } from 'react';


function Counter(props) {

  const [count, setCount] =
useState(props.initialValue || 0);


  const increment = () => {

    setCount(count + 1);


    if (count + 1 === 15) {

      alert('Counter has reached 15!');
```

```
      }

   };



   // ... (rest of the code)

}



export default Counter;
```

In this code:

- Inside the `increment` function, we check if the new counter value will be 15.

- If it is, we display an alert message using `alert()`.

Save the file and try incrementing the counter. When the counter value reaches 15, you should see an alert message.

Conditional Rendering in the Counter Component

Let's add another feature to our counter application that displays a message when the counter value is even or odd.

Modify the `Counter` component code as follows:

```
import React, { useState } from 'react';
```

```
function Counter(props) {

  const [count, setCount] =
useState(props.initialValue || 0);



  // ... (other code)


  return (



    {/* ... (other elements) */}


    {count % 2 === 0 ? (


Counter is even


    ) : (


Counter is odd


    )}
```

```
  );

}


export default Counter;
```

In this code:

- We use a ternary operator to conditionally render a paragraph element based on whether the `count` value is even or odd.

- If `count % 2 === 0` (i.e., the remainder when `count` is divided by 2 is 0), we render the "Counter is even" message.

- Otherwise, we render the "Counter is odd" message.

Save the file and observe the changes in your browser. The counter application should now display a message indicating whether the counter value is even or odd.

Building a Simple To-Do List Application

Let's build another simple application to further solidify our understanding of React development. We'll create a basic to-do list application that allows users to add and remove items from a list.

Create a new file named `TodoList.js` in the `src` folder and add the following code:

```
import React, { useState } from 'react';

function TodoList() {

  const [todos, setTodos] = useState([]);

  const [newTodo, setNewTodo] =
useState('');


  const addTodo = () => {

    if (newTodo.trim() !== '') {

      setTodos([...todos, newTodo]);

      setNewTodo('');

    }

  };


  const removeTodo = (index) => {

    const updatedTodos = todos.filter((_, i)
=> i !== index);

    setTodos(updatedTodos);

  };
```

```
return (
```

To-Do List

{newTodo} setNewTodo(e.target.value)}

/>

Add

{todos.map((todo, index) => (

•

{todo}

removeTodo(index)}>Remove

```
        ) ) }




    ) ;

}



export default TodoList;
```

In this code:

- We initialize the `todos` state variable to an empty array using `useState([])`. This array will store our to-do items.

- We initialize the `newTodo` state variable to an empty string using `useState('')`. This variable will store the text entered by the user in the input field.

- The `addTodo` function adds the `newTodo` to the `todos` array and clears the input field.

- The `removeTodo` function removes the to-do item at the specified index from the `todos` array.

- We render an input field, an "Add" button, and an unordered list to display the to-do items.

- We use the map() method to iterate over the todos array and render a list item for each to-do item.

- Each list item includes the to-do text and a "Remove" button that calls the removeTodo function when clicked.

Now, let's import and use this TodoList component in our App.js file:

```
import React from 'react';

import './App.css';

import TodoList from './TodoList';


function App() {

  return (




  );

}
```

```
export default App;
```

In this code:

- We import the `TodoList` component from `./TodoList`.

- We render the `TodoList` component within the `App` component.

Save the files and observe the changes in your browser. You should now see a to-do list application. You can enter text in the input field and click "Add" to add it to the list. You can also click the "Remove" button next to each item to remove it from the list.

These simple applications demonstrate the fundamental concepts of React development, including creating components, managing state, handling events, and conditional rendering. As you progress through this book, you'll explore more advanced React features and build increasingly complex and interactive applications. With React as your front-end toolkit, you'll be well-equipped to create captivating web experiences that delight users and elevate your MERN stack applications to new heights.

Chapter Ten: Managing State in React with Hooks

In the previous chapters, we embarked on our React journey, learning about JSX, components, props, and building our first React applications. As our applications grow in complexity, managing the data that drives our user interface becomes increasingly crucial. This data, often referred to as state, represents the dynamic aspects of our application, such as user input, loading status, or the visibility of elements. In this chapter, we'll explore a powerful feature introduced in React 16.8 called Hooks, which revolutionize how we manage state and other React features within functional components.

Hooks: A New Way to Manage State

Before Hooks, managing state in React was primarily done within class components. Class components provided methods like `this.state` and `this.setState` to initialize and update state. However, class components could be verbose and sometimes lead to confusing code, especially when dealing with complex state management logic.

Hooks offer a more elegant and concise way to manage state and other React features within functional components. Hooks are functions that let you "hook into" React state and lifecycle features from within functional components, eliminating the need for class components in many cases.

The `useState` Hook: Managing Simple State

The `useState` Hook is the most fundamental Hook for managing state in React. It allows you to add state to a functional component and provides a way to update that state.

Let's illustrate the useState Hook with a simple example. Suppose we want to create a counter component that allows the user to increment and decrement a counter value. We can define a functional component like this:

```
import React, { useState } from 'react';

function Counter() {

  const [count, setCount] = useState(0);


  const increment = () => {

    setCount(count + 1);

  };


  const decrement = () => {

    setCount(count - 1);

  };


  return (

    <div>

      <p>Count: {count}</p>
```

```
        <button
onClick={increment}>Increment</button>

        <button
onClick={decrement}>Decrement</button>

    </div>

  );

}



export default Counter;
```

In this code:

- We import the useState Hook from React.

- We initialize the count state variable to 0 using
  useState(0). useState returns an array containing
  two elements: the current state value (in this case, count)
  and a function to update that state (in this case,
  setCount).

- We define two functions, increment and decrement,
  that update the count state using setCount.

- We render the count value and two buttons that call the
  increment and decrement functions when clicked.

When this component is rendered, it will display the counter value
and two buttons. Clicking the "Increment" button will increase the
counter value, and clicking the "Decrement" button will decrease
it.

Updating State with the `useState` Hook

The `setCount` function returned by `useState` is used to update the state variable. When you call `setCount` with a new value, React re-renders the component, reflecting the updated state in the UI.

In the `Counter` component example, we call `setCount(count + 1)` to increment the counter and `setCount(count - 1)` to decrement it.

Using the `useState` Hook with Objects

The `useState` Hook can also be used to manage state that's represented by an object. Suppose we want to create a component that allows the user to enter their name and email address. We can define a functional component like this:

```
import React, { useState } from 'react';



function UserForm() {

  const [user, setUser] = useState({ name:
'', email: '' });



  const handleChange = (event) => {

    setUser({ ...user, [event.target.name]:
event.target.value });

  };
```

```jsx
  return (
    <form>
      <div>
        <label htmlFor="name">Name:</label>
        <input
          type="text"
          id="name"
          name="name"
          value={user.name}
          onChange={handleChange}
        />
      </div>
      <div>
        <label
htmlFor="email">Email:</label>
        <input
          type="email"
          id="email"
          name="email"
```

```
      value={user.email}

      onChange={handleChange}

    />

  </div>

  <button type="submit">Submit</button>

  </form>

  );

}


export default UserForm;
```

In this code:

- We initialize the `user` state variable to an object with `name` and `email` properties, both initially set to empty strings.

- The `handleChange` function updates the `user` state whenever an input field changes. We use the spread syntax (`...user`) to create a new object that copies the existing `user` state and then updates the specific property that corresponds to the changed input field.

The useEffect Hook: Managing Side Effects

The `useEffect` Hook allows you to perform side effects in functional components. Side effects are actions that affect something outside the scope of the function, such as fetching data from an API, subscribing to events, or manually manipulating the DOM.

In class components, side effects were typically handled in lifecycle methods like `componentDidMount`, `componentDidUpdate`, and `componentWillUnmount`. The `useEffect` Hook provides a way to handle these side effects in a more declarative and concise way within functional components.

Let's illustrate the `useEffect` Hook with an example. Suppose we want to fetch data from an API when the component mounts and update the component's state with the fetched data. We can define a functional component like this:

```
import React, { useState, useEffect } from
'react';


function DataFetcher() {

  const [data, setData] = useState(null);


  useEffect(() => {

    const fetchData = async () => {

      const response = await
fetch('https://api.example.com/data');

      const jsonData = await
response.json();
```

```
      setData(jsonData);

   };


   fetchData();

}, []);


return (

   <div>

      {data ? (

         <ul>

            {data.map((item) => (

               <li
key={item.id}>{item.name}</li>

            ))}

         </ul>

      ) : (

         <p>Loading data...</p>

      )}

   </div>

);
```

```
}


export default DataFetcher;
```

In this code:

- We initialize the data state variable to null.

- We use the useEffect Hook to fetch data from the API when the component mounts.

- The useEffect Hook takes two arguments: a callback function and a dependency array.

- The callback function is executed after every render of the component.

- The dependency array specifies which values the useEffect Hook should depend on. If any of the values in the dependency array change between renders, the callback function will be executed again.

- In our example, we pass an empty dependency array ([]), which means that the callback function will only be executed once, when the component mounts.

- Inside the callback function, we define an asynchronous function fetchData that fetches the data from the API and updates the data state with the fetched data.

- We call fetchData at the end of the callback function.

- We conditionally render either a list of data items or a "Loading data..." message based on whether the `data` state is `null` or not.

Using the `useEffect` Hook with Cleanup

Sometimes, side effects require cleanup, such as unsubscribing from events or clearing timers. The `useEffect` Hook provides a way to handle cleanup by returning a cleanup function from the callback function.

The cleanup function will be executed when the component unmounts or when the `useEffect` Hook is re-executed due to a change in the dependency array.

Let's illustrate this with an example. Suppose we want to subscribe to an event when the component mounts and unsubscribe from it when the component unmounts. We can define a functional component like this:

```
import React, { useState, useEffect } from
'react';



function EventSubscriber() {

  const [message, setMessage] =
useState('');



  useEffect(() => {

    const handleEvent = (event) => {

      setMessage(event.data);
```

```
  };


  window.addEventListener('myEvent',
handleEvent);


  return () => {

    window.removeEventListener('myEvent',
handleEvent);

  };

}, []);


  return (

    <div>

      <p>Message: {message}</p>

    </div>

  );

}


export default EventSubscriber;
```

In this code:

- We initialize the `message` state variable to an empty string.

- We use the `useEffect` Hook to subscribe to the `myEvent` event when the component mounts.

- Inside the callback function, we define an event handler function `handleEvent` that updates the `message` state with the event data.

- We attach the `handleEvent` function to the `myEvent` event using `window.addEventListener`.

- We return a cleanup function from the callback function. The cleanup function removes the event listener using `window.removeEventListener`.

- When the component unmounts, the cleanup function will be executed, ensuring that we unsubscribe from the event and prevent memory leaks.

Using the `useEffect` Hook with Dependencies

As mentioned earlier, the dependency array in the `useEffect` Hook specifies which values the Hook should depend on. If any of the values in the dependency array change between renders, the callback function will be executed again.

Let's illustrate this with an example. Suppose we want to fetch data from an API whenever a `userId` prop changes. We can define a functional component like this:

```
import React, { useState, useEffect } from 'react';
```

```
function UserDataProvider(props) {

  const [userData, setUserData] =
useState(null);


  useEffect(() => {

    const fetchData = async () => {

      const response = await fetch(

`https://api.example.com/users/${props.userI
d}`

      );

      const jsonData = await
response.json();

      setUserData(jsonData);

    };


    fetchData();

  }, [props.userId]);


  return (

    <div>
```

```
    {userData ? (

      <p>User name: {userData.name}</p>

    ) : (

      <p>Loading user data...</p>

    )}

  </div>

  );

}



export default UserDataProvider;
```

In this code:

- We initialize the `userData` state variable to `null`.

- We use the `useEffect` Hook to fetch user data from the API whenever the `userId` prop changes.

- We pass `props.userId` in the dependency array, which means that the callback function will be executed whenever the `userId` prop changes.

- Inside the callback function, we define an asynchronous function `fetchData` that fetches the user data from the API and updates the `userData` state with the fetched data.

- We call `fetchData` at the end of the callback function.

- We conditionally render either the user's name or a "Loading user data..." message based on whether the `userData` state is `null` or not.

Other Built-in Hooks

Besides `useState` and `useEffect`, React provides several other built-in Hooks that offer various functionalities:

- `useContext`: Allows you to access the value of a React context from within a functional component.

- `useReducer`: Provides a way to manage complex state logic using a reducer function.

- `useCallback`: Memoizes a callback function, preventing unnecessary re-creations of the function.

- `useMemo`: Memoizes the result of a function, preventing unnecessary re-computations of the function.

- `useRef`: Creates a mutable ref object that persists across renders of the component.

- `useImperativeHandle`: Allows you to customize the instance value exposed by a component to parent components when using `ref`.

- `useLayoutEffect`: Similar to `useEffect`, but the callback function is executed synchronously after all DOM mutations.

- `useDebugValue`: Allows you to display a label for custom Hooks in React DevTools.

Custom Hooks: Reusability and Abstraction

One of the powerful features of Hooks is the ability to create custom Hooks. Custom Hooks allow you to extract reusable stateful logic from your components, making your code more organized, maintainable, and testable.

A custom Hook is essentially a JavaScript function that uses one or more built-in Hooks and returns a value or a set of values that can be used by other components.

Let's illustrate this with an example. Suppose we want to create a custom Hook that fetches data from an API and provides the data and a loading status to the components that use it. We can define a custom Hook like this:

```javascript
import { useState, useEffect } from 'react';


function useFetchData(url) {

  const [data, setData] = useState(null);

  const [loading, setLoading] =
useState(true);


  useEffect(() => {

    const fetchData = async () => {

      const response = await fetch(url);

      const jsonData = await
response.json();

      setData(jsonData);
```

```
      setLoading(false);

    };


    fetchData();

  }, [url]);


  return { data, loading };

}


export default useFetchData;
```

In this code:

- We define a custom Hook named `useFetchData` that takes a URL as an argument.

- We initialize the `data` and `loading` state variables using `useState`.

- We use the `useEffect` Hook to fetch data from the API when the component mounts or when the URL changes.

- We return an object containing the `data` and `loading` values.

Now, we can use this custom Hook in any component that needs to fetch data from an API:

```
import React from 'react';

import useFetchData from './useFetchData';


function MyComponent() {

  const { data, loading } =
useFetchData('https://api.example.com/data')
;


  return (

    <div>

      {loading ? (

        <p>Loading data...</p>

      ) : (

        <ul>

          {data.map((item) => (

            <li
key={item.id}>{item.name}</li>

          ))}

        </ul>
```

```
    ) }

    </div>

  );

}


export default MyComponent;
```

In this code:

- We import the `useFetchData` custom Hook.

- We call `useFetchData` with the API URL and destructure the returned `data` and `loading` values.

- We conditionally render either a "Loading data..." message or a list of data items based on the `loading` status.

Rules of Hooks

Hooks have a few rules that you need to follow to ensure that they work correctly:

- **Only Call Hooks at the Top Level:** You can only call Hooks from React function components or custom Hooks. You cannot call Hooks from within loops, conditions, or nested functions.

- **Only Call Hooks from React Functions:** You can only call Hooks from React function components or custom

Hooks. You cannot call Hooks from regular JavaScript functions.

Conclusion

Hooks have significantly improved the way we manage state and other React features within functional components. They offer a more elegant, concise, and reusable approach compared to traditional class components. By mastering Hooks, you can write cleaner, more maintainable, and more testable React code. As you continue your React journey, you'll discover the versatility of Hooks and how they can empower you to build sophisticated and dynamic user interfaces with ease.

Chapter Eleven: Fetching Data with React and Axios

In the previous chapter, we explored the intricacies of state management in React using Hooks, empowering us to build dynamic and interactive user interfaces that respond to changes in data. Now, it's time to expand our horizons and connect our React applications to the outside world by fetching data from external sources, such as APIs. In this chapter, we'll learn how to make HTTP requests from our React components using Axios, a popular JavaScript library that simplifies the process of interacting with APIs. We'll explore various techniques for fetching data, handling loading states, displaying data in our UI, and gracefully managing errors. By the end of this chapter, you'll be equipped with the skills to build data-driven React applications that seamlessly integrate with external APIs.

Axios: A Powerful HTTP Client for JavaScript

Axios is a promise-based HTTP client for JavaScript that can be used in both the browser and Node.js environments. It provides a simple and elegant API for making HTTP requests, handling responses, and managing errors.

Compared to the built-in `fetch` API in JavaScript, Axios offers several advantages:

- **Automatic JSON Transformation:** Axios automatically transforms JSON data received from the server into JavaScript objects, eliminating the need for manual parsing.

- **Error Handling:** Axios provides a more streamlined way to handle errors compared to `fetch`. It throws errors for network problems and HTTP errors, making it easier to catch and handle errors in your code.

- **Interceptors:** Axios allows you to intercept requests or responses before they are handled. This can be useful for adding headers, logging requests, or modifying responses globally.

- **Built-in Support for Progress Tracking:** Axios has built-in support for tracking the progress of uploads and downloads, which can be useful for displaying progress bars or other visual indicators.

Installing Axios

Before we can start using Axios, we need to install it. Open your terminal or command prompt, navigate to the root directory of your React project, and run the following command:

```
npm install axios
```

This command will download and install the Axios library and its dependencies.

Making a GET Request with Axios

Let's start with a simple example of fetching data from an API using Axios. Suppose we want to fetch a list of users from the JSONPlaceholder API, a free online REST API for testing and prototyping.

Create a new file named UserList.js in your src folder and add the following code:

```javascript
import React, { useState, useEffect } from
'react';

import axios from 'axios';


function UserList() {

  const [users, setUsers] = useState([]);

  const [loading, setLoading] =
useState(true);

  const [error, setError] = useState(null);


  useEffect(() => {

    const fetchUsers = async () => {

      try {

        const response = await axios.get(

'https://jsonplaceholder.typicode.com/users'

        );

        setUsers(response.data);

        setLoading(false);

      } catch (error) {

        setError(error);
```

```
      setLoading(false);

    }

  };


  fetchUsers();
}, []);


if (loading) {
  return
Loading users...
;
  }


if (error) {
  return
Error: {error.message}
;
  }


  return (
```

```
                {users.map((user) => (


    •



                {user.name} ({user.email})




        ))}



    );

}



export default UserList;
```

In this code:

- We import the `axios` library.

- We initialize three state variables: `users` to store the fetched user data, `loading` to track the loading status, and `error` to store any errors that occur during the fetching process.

- We use the `useEffect` Hook to fetch the user data when the component mounts.

- Inside the `useEffect` Hook, we define an asynchronous function `fetchUsers` that makes a GET request to the JSONPlaceholder API using `axios.get()`.

- We wrap the `axios.get()` call in a `try...catch` block to handle potential errors.

- If the request is successful, we update the `users` state with the fetched data and set `loading` to `false`.

- If an error occurs, we update the `error` state with the error object and set `loading` to `false`.

- We conditionally render different content based on the `loading` and `error` states.

- If `loading` is `true`, we display a "Loading users..." message.

- If `error` is not `null`, we display an error message.

- If both `loading` and `error` are `false`, we render a list of users using the `users` state.

Making a POST Request with Axios

Let's now look at an example of making a POST request with Axios to send data to an API. Suppose we have a form where the user can enter their name and email address, and we want to send this data to the JSONPlaceholder API to create a new user.

Create a new file named `UserForm.js` in your `src` folder and add the following code:

```
import React, { useState } from 'react';

import axios from 'axios';


function UserForm() {

  const [name, setName] = useState('');

  const [email, setEmail] = useState('');

  const [submitting, setSubmitting] =
useState(false);

  const [error, setError] = useState(null);


  const handleSubmit = async (event) => {

    event.preventDefault();


    try {

      setSubmitting(true);

      const response = await axios.post(

'https://jsonplaceholder.typicode.com/users'
,

        {

          name: name,
```

```
        email: email,

    }

  );

  console.log('User created:',
response.data);

  setName('');

  setEmail('');

  setSubmitting(false);

} catch (error) {

  setError(error);

  setSubmitting(false);

}

};


return (
```

In this code:

- We initialize four state variables: `name` and `email` to store the user's input, `submitting` to track the submission status, and `error` to store any errors that occur during the submission process.

- The `handleSubmit` function is called when the form is submitted.

- Inside `handleSubmit`, we prevent the default form submission behavior using `event.preventDefault()`.

- We set `submitting` to `true` to indicate that the form is being submitted.

- We make a POST request to the JSONPlaceholder API using `axios.post()`, passing the user's name and email as data.

- If the request is successful, we log the created user data to the console, clear the input fields, and set `submitting` to `false`.

- If an error occurs, we update the `error` state with the error object and set `submitting` to `false`.

- We render a form with input fields for the user's name and email, a submit button, and an error message (if there's an error).

- We disable the submit button while the form is being submitted.

Making Other Types of Requests with Axios

Axios supports other HTTP methods besides GET and POST, such as PUT, DELETE, PATCH, and more. You can use the corresponding methods on the `axios` object to make these requests.

For example, to make a PUT request to update a user's data, you would use `axios.put()`:

```
const response = await axios.put(

`https://jsonplaceholder.typicode.com/users/
${userId}`,

  {

    name: newName,

    email: newEmail,

  }

);
```

Using Axios Interceptors

Axios interceptors allow you to intercept requests or responses before they are handled. This can be useful for adding headers, logging requests, or modifying responses globally.

To add an interceptor, you use the `interceptors` property on the `axios` object. For example, to add a request interceptor that adds an authorization header to every request, you would do the following:

```
axios.interceptors.request.use((config) => {

  config.headers.Authorization = `Bearer
${token}`;
```

```
    return config;

});
```

This interceptor will add an `Authorization` header with the value `Bearer ${token}` to every request made using Axios.

Handling Loading States

When fetching data from an API, it's important to provide feedback to the user about the loading status. This can be done by displaying a loading indicator or message while the data is being fetched.

In the `UserList` component example, we used the `loading` state variable to track the loading status and conditionally rendered a "Loading users..." message while the data was being fetched.

Displaying Data in the UI

Once you've fetched data from an API, you can display it in your React components using JSX. In the `UserList` component example, we used the `map()` method to iterate over the `users` array and render a list item for each user.

Handling Errors

When fetching data from an API, errors can occur due to various reasons, such as network problems, server errors, or invalid requests. It's crucial to handle these errors gracefully and provide informative error messages to the user.

In the `UserList` and `UserForm` component examples, we used the `error` state variable to store any errors that occurred during

147

the fetching or submission process. We then conditionally rendered an error message based on the `error` state.

Using Async/Await with Axios

Axios supports async/await, which allows you to write asynchronous code that looks and behaves like synchronous code. This can make your code easier to read and understand.

In the `UserList` and `UserForm` component examples, we used async/await to make the API requests and handle the responses.

Conclusion

Fetching data from external APIs is a fundamental aspect of building modern web applications. Axios provides a powerful and convenient way to make HTTP requests from your React components, handle responses, and manage errors. By mastering Axios and the techniques we've explored in this chapter, you'll be well-equipped to build data-driven React applications that seamlessly integrate with external services and provide rich and dynamic user experiences. Remember, the ability to fetch and display data from APIs opens up a world of possibilities for your React applications, allowing you to create applications that are both informative and engaging.

Chapter Twelve: Routing in React with React Router

In the previous chapters, we've explored the core building blocks of React, including components, state management, and fetching data from APIs. We've built applications that render a single view or page. However, as our applications grow in complexity, we often need to navigate between multiple views or pages, creating a more interactive and user-friendly experience. This is where routing comes into play. Routing allows us to define different paths or URLs within our application and associate them with specific components or views. In this chapter, we'll delve into the world of routing in React using React Router, a popular library that provides the tools and components necessary to implement navigation and routing in our React applications.

React Router: The Navigation Solution for React

React Router is a powerful and widely used library for implementing routing and navigation in React applications. It provides a declarative way to define routes, handle navigation, and manage the display of different components based on the current URL.

React Router's core concept is the idea of routes. A route defines a mapping between a URL path and a component that should be rendered when that path is accessed. For example, we might have a route that maps the path / (the root path) to a `Home` component and another route that maps the path `/about` to an `About` component.

React Router provides several components that make it easy to define and manage routes:

- `<BrowserRouter>`: This component provides the context for routing and navigation within your application. It's typically used at the top level of your application, wrapping all the components that need access to routing functionalities.

- `<Routes>`: This component acts as a container for defining individual routes. It's used within the `<BrowserRouter>` component.

- `<Route>`: This component defines a single route. It takes two main props: `path`, which specifies the URL path for the route, and `element`, which specifies the component to be rendered when the path is matched.

Installing React Router

Before we can start using React Router, we need to install it. Open your terminal or command prompt, navigate to the root directory of your React project, and run the following command:

```
npm install react-router-dom
```

This command will download and install the `react-router-dom` package, which contains the components and functionalities needed for routing in web applications.

Setting Up Basic Routing

Let's start with a simple example of setting up basic routing in a React application. We'll create a small application with two pages: a home page and an about page.

Create a new file named `App.js` in your `src` folder and add the following code:

```javascript
import React from 'react';

import { BrowserRouter, Routes, Route, Link
} from 'react-router-dom';


function Home() {

  return (
```

Home

Welcome to the home page!

```
    );

}


function About() {

    return (
```

About

This is the about page.

```
  );

}


function App() {

  return (
```

-

-

```
            } />

            } />



        );
    }
```

```
export default App;
```

In this code:

- We import the necessary components from `react-router-dom`.

- We define two functional components, `Home` and `About`, which represent the content of our two pages.

- In the `App` component, we wrap everything in a `<BrowserRouter>` component to provide the routing context.

- We create a navigation bar with links to the home and about pages using the `<Link>` component. The `to` prop of the `<Link>` component specifies the URL path to navigate to when the link is clicked.

- We define the routes using the `<Routes>` and `<Route>` components.

- The `<Route path="/" element={<Home />}` route maps the root path `/` to the `Home` component.

- The `<Route path="/about" element={<About />}` route maps the path `/about` to the `About` component.

Save the file and start your development server (if it's not already running). You should now see the home page with a navigation bar. Clicking the "About" link in the navigation bar will navigate you to the about page, and clicking the "Home" link will take you back to the home page.

Nested Routes

React Router allows you to define nested routes, which are routes that are nested within other routes. This can be useful for creating hierarchical navigation structures, such as a dashboard with sub-sections or a blog with categories and individual posts.

Let's illustrate nested routes with an example. Suppose we want to add a dashboard section to our application with two sub-sections: profile and settings.

Modify the App.js file as follows:

```
import React from 'react';

import {

    BrowserRouter,

    Routes,

    Route,

    Link,

    Outlet,

} from 'react-router-dom';


// ... (Home and About components)


function Dashboard() {
```

```
return (
```

Dashboard

•

•

```
    );

}


function DashboardProfile() {

  return (
```

Profile

This is your profile page.

```
  );

}


function DashboardSettings() {

  return (
```

Settings

This is the settings page.

```
    );

}


function App() {

    return (



            {/* ... (navigation bar) */}
```

```
            {/*  ...  (Home  and  About  routes)
*/}



         }>

           }  />

           }  />











   );

}



export  default  App;
```

In this code:

- We define a `Dashboard` component that acts as a parent component for the dashboard sub-sections.

- We use the `<Outlet>` component within the Dashboard component to render the content of the nested routes.

- We define two nested routes within the Dashboard route:

- `<Route path="profile" element={<DashboardProfile />}>` maps the path `/dashboard/profile` to the `DashboardProfile` component.

- `<Route path="settings" element={<DashboardSettings />}>` maps the path `/dashboard/settings` to the `DashboardSettings` component.

Save the file and observe the changes in your browser. You should now see a "Dashboard" link in the navigation bar. Clicking it will take you to the dashboard page, which will display a navigation bar for the profile and settings sub-sections. Clicking the links in the dashboard navigation bar will render the corresponding sub-section content within the `<Outlet>` component.

Dynamic Routes

React Router allows you to define dynamic routes, which are routes that have parameters in their paths. Parameters are placeholders in the URL that can capture values, such as user IDs, product IDs, or category names.

Let's illustrate dynamic routes with an example. Suppose we want to add a user details page to our application that displays information about a specific user based on their ID.

Modify the `App.js` file as follows:

```
import React from 'react';

import {

  BrowserRouter,

  Routes,

  Route,

  Link,

  useParams,

} from 'react-router-dom';


// ... (other components)


function UserDetails() {

  const { userId } = useParams();


  return (
```

User Details

```
User ID: {userId}



  );

}



function App() {

  return (



        {/* ... (navigation bar) */}
```

```
        {/* ... (other routes) */}


    } />



    );

}



export default App;
```

In this code:

- We define a `UserDetails` component that displays the details of a specific user.

- We use the `useParams` Hook within the `UserDetails` component to access the route parameters. The `useParams` Hook returns an object where the keys are the parameter names and the values are the parameter values.

- We define a dynamic route `<Route path="/users/:userId"`

element={<UserDetails />} /> that maps the path /users/:userId to the UserDetails component. The :userId part of the path indicates a parameter named userId.

Save the file and try navigating to a URL like /users/1 or /users/2. You should see the UserDetails component rendered with the user ID displayed.

Programmatic Navigation

React Router allows you to navigate programmatically, meaning you can trigger navigation from within your components using JavaScript code. This can be useful for scenarios like redirecting the user after a form submission or navigating to a specific page based on user interactions.

To navigate programmatically, you can use the useNavigate Hook. The useNavigate Hook returns a function that you can call to navigate to a different URL.

Let's illustrate programmatic navigation with an example. Suppose we want to redirect the user to the home page after they submit a form.

Modify the UserForm component (from the previous chapter) as follows:

```
import React, { useState } from 'react';

import axios from 'axios';

import { useNavigate } from 'react-router-dom';
```

```
function UserForm() {

  // ... (other state variables)


  const navigate = useNavigate();


  const handleSubmit = async (event) => {

    // ... (form submission logic)


    if (/* form submission successful */) {

      navigate('/'); // Redirect to the home
page

    }

  };


  // ... (rest of the component)

}


export default UserForm;
```

In this code:

- We import the `useNavigate` Hook from `react-router-dom`.

- We call the `useNavigate` Hook to get the `navigate` function.

- Inside the `handleSubmit` function, after the form submission is successful, we call `navigate('/')` to redirect the user to the home page.

404 Not Found Page

When a user navigates to a URL that doesn't match any defined routes, it's good practice to display a 404 Not Found page. This provides a user-friendly experience and informs the user that the requested page doesn't exist.

To create a 404 Not Found page, you can define a route with a wildcard path * that matches any URL that hasn't been matched by other routes.

Modify the `App.js` file as follows:

```
import React from 'react';

import { BrowserRouter, Routes, Route, Link
} from 'react-router-dom';



// ... (other components)



function NotFound() {

  return (
```

404 Not Found

The page you requested could not be found.

```
  );
}


function App() {
  return (




        {/* ... (navigation bar) */}
```

```
        {/* ... (other routes) */}



      } />
```

```
  );
```

```
}
```

```
export default App;
```

In this code:

- We define a `NotFound` component that represents the 404 Not Found page.

- We define a route `<Route path="*" element={<NotFound />} />` that maps any unmatched URL to the `NotFound` component.

Save the file and try navigating to a URL that doesn't exist, such as `/invalid-path`. You should see the `NotFound` component rendered.

Protected Routes

In many applications, you might have certain routes that should only be accessible to authenticated users. For example, you might have a profile page or a dashboard that requires the user to be logged in to view.

React Router doesn't provide built-in functionality for protected routes, but you can easily implement them using custom logic.

One common approach is to create a higher-order component (HOC) that wraps the protected component and checks if the user is authenticated before rendering it. If the user is not authenticated, the HOC can redirect them to the login page.

Here's an example of a simple HOC for protected routes:

```
import React from 'react';

import { Navigate } from 'react-router-dom';



function withAuth(Component) {

  return function
AuthenticatedComponent(props) {

    const isAuthenticated = /* check if user
is authenticated */;


    if (isAuthenticated) {

      return ;
```

```
    } else {

        return ;

    }

  };

}



export default withAuth;
```

In this code:

- We define a function `withAuth` that takes a component as an argument and returns a new component.

- The returned component checks if the user is authenticated using the `isAuthenticated` variable (you'll need to implement the authentication logic yourself).

- If the user is authenticated, it renders the original component with the passed props.

- If the user is not authenticated, it redirects them to the login page using the `<Navigate>` component.

You can then use this HOC to wrap your protected components:

```
import React from 'react';

import withAuth from './withAuth';
```

```
function Profile() {

  return (
```

Profile

```
    {/* ... profile content */}



  );

}



const AuthenticatedProfile =
withAuth(Profile);



export default AuthenticatedProfile;
```

In this code:

- We import the `withAuth` HOC.

- We wrap the `Profile` component with `withAuth` to create a new component `AuthenticatedProfile`.

- When you render `AuthenticatedProfile`, it will check if the user is authenticated before rendering the `Profile` component.

Customizing the Link Component

React Router's `<Link>` component provides basic styling for links, but you might want to customize the appearance of your links to match your application's design.

You can customize the `<Link>` component by passing a `className` prop or by using styled-components or other CSS-in-JS libraries.

Here's an example of customizing the `<Link>` component using a `className` prop:

```
import React from 'react';

import { Link } from 'react-router-dom';

import './MyLink.css';



function MyLink(props) {

    return
```

In this code:

- We create a custom component `MyLink` that wraps the `<Link>` component.

- We pass a `className` prop to the `<Link>` component, which applies the CSS class `my-link` to the link element.

177

You can then use the MyLink component instead of the standard <Link> component in your application:

```
import React from 'react';

import MyLink from './MyLink';


function App() {

  return (
```

-

          Home

-

          About

```
      {/* ... other content */}



    );

}



export default App;
```

Using React Router with Redux

If you're using Redux for state management in your React
application, you can integrate React Router with Redux to manage
your application's routing state within the Redux store.

There are libraries like `connected-react-router` that
provide seamless integration between React Router and Redux.

Conclusion

React Router is an indispensable tool for building modern web
applications with React. Its declarative approach to routing, nested
routes, dynamic routes, programmatic navigation, and other

features make it easy to create complex and interactive navigation structures. By mastering React Router, you can enhance the user experience of your applications and build applications that are both intuitive and engaging. Remember, routing is a fundamental aspect of web development, and React Router provides the tools and components you need to implement routing effectively in your React applications, ensuring a seamless and enjoyable user experience.

Chapter Thirteen: Building Forms in React

Forms are the backbone of user interaction in web applications. They're the gateways through which users provide information, make choices, and initiate actions. From simple login forms to complex multi-step surveys, forms are essential for gathering data, processing requests, and enabling user engagement. In this chapter, we'll delve into the world of building forms in React, exploring the techniques and best practices for creating forms that are both user-friendly and efficient. We'll learn how to handle user input, manage form state, validate data, and submit forms to our back-end API, empowering us to create robust and interactive forms that seamlessly integrate with our MERN stack applications.

Controlled Components: Taming User Input

React's approach to handling user input in forms revolves around the concept of controlled components. A controlled component is a form element whose value is controlled by React's state. This means that the value of the form element is not directly manipulated by the user's input but is instead managed by React, ensuring that the form's state accurately reflects the user's actions.

To create a controlled component, you bind the value of the form element to a state variable and update that state variable whenever the user interacts with the form element. Let's illustrate this with a simple example of a text input field:

```
import React, { useState } from 'react';


function MyForm() {

  const [name, setName] = useState('');
```

```
const handleChange = (event) => {

  setName(event.target.value);

};



  return (
```

In this code:

- We initialize the `name` state variable to an empty string using `useState('')`.

- The `handleChange` function is called whenever the user types into the input field. It updates the `name` state variable with the current value of the input field using `setName(event.target.value)`.

- The `value` attribute of the input field is bound to the `name` state variable. This ensures that the value of the input field is always in sync with React's state.

As the user types into the input field, the `handleChange` function updates the `name` state variable, which in turn updates the value displayed in the input field. This creates a controlled flow of data where React manages the state of the form element.

Handling Form Submission

Form submission is a crucial aspect of form handling. It's the mechanism through which the data entered by the user is sent to the back-end for processing. In React, you typically handle form submission using an event handler attached to the form's `onSubmit` event.

Let's expand our previous example to handle form submission:

```javascript
import React, { useState } from 'react';


function MyForm() {

  const [name, setName] = useState('');


  const handleChange = (event) => {

    setName(event.target.value);

  };


  const handleSubmit = (event) => {

    event.preventDefault(); // Prevent
default form submission


    console.log('Name:', name); // Log the
form data


    // TODO: Send form data to the back-end
```

```
};
```

```
return (
```

In this code:

- We define a `handleSubmit` function that is called when the form is submitted.

- Inside `handleSubmit`, we use `event.preventDefault()` to prevent the default form submission behavior, which would cause the page to reload.

- We log the form data to the console for demonstration purposes. In a real application, you would typically send the form data to your back-end API for processing.

Multiple Form Fields

Handling multiple form fields is a common requirement in web applications. You can apply the same controlled component approach to each form field, binding its value to a separate state variable and updating that state variable whenever the field changes.

Let's expand our form to include an email field:

```
import React, { useState } from 'react';
```

```
function MyForm() {

  const [name, setName] = useState('');

  const [email, setEmail] = useState('');


  const handleChange = (event) => {

    const { name, value } = event.target;


    if (name === 'name') {

      setName(value);

    } else if (name === 'email') {

      setEmail(value);

    }

  };


  const handleSubmit = (event) => {

    event.preventDefault();


    console.log('Name:', name);

    console.log('Email:', email);
```

```
  // TODO: Send form data to the back-end

};


return (
```

In this code:

- We initialize two state variables, `name` and `email`, to store the values of the name and email fields, respectively.

- The `handleChange` function now handles changes to both fields. We use `event.target.name` to identify which field has changed and update the corresponding state variable.

Checkboxes and Radio Buttons

Checkboxes and radio buttons require a slightly different approach compared to text input fields. Instead of binding their value to a state variable, you typically bind their `checked` attribute to a boolean state variable that indicates whether the checkbox or radio button is checked.

Let's add a checkbox to our form to allow the user to subscribe to a newsletter:

```
import React, { useState } from 'react';
```

```
function MyForm() {

   // ... (other state variables)

   const [newsletter, setNewsletter] =
   useState(false);


   const handleChange = (event) => {

      // ... (handling for name and email
   fields)


      if (event.target.name === 'newsletter')
   {

         setNewsletter(event.target.checked);

      }

   };


   // ... (handleSubmit function)


   return (
```

In this code:

- We initialize the `newsletter` state variable to `false` using `useState(false)`.

- The `handleChange` function handles changes to the checkbox. We update the `newsletter` state variable with the `checked` value of the checkbox using `setNewsletter(event.target.checked)`.

- The `checked` attribute of the checkbox is bound to the `newsletter` state variable.

Select Elements

Select elements allow users to choose from a list of options. To create a controlled select element, you bind its `value` attribute to a state variable that represents the selected option.

Let's add a select element to our form to allow the user to choose their favorite color:

```
import React, { useState } from 'react';


function MyForm() {

  // ... (other state variables)

  const [color, setColor] = useState('');


  const handleChange = (event) => {

    // ... (handling for name, email, and
newsletter fields)
```

```
    if (event.target.name === 'color') {

        setColor(event.target.value);

    }

};


// ... (handleSubmit function)


return (
```

In this code:

- We initialize the `color` state variable to an empty string using `useState('')`.

- The `handleChange` function handles changes to the select element. We update the `color` state variable with the selected option's value using `setColor(event.target.value)`.

- The `value` attribute of the select element is bound to the `color` state variable.

Textarea Elements

Textarea elements allow users to enter multi-line text. To create a controlled textarea element, you bind its `value` attribute to a state variable that represents the text entered by the user.

Let's add a textarea to our form to allow the user to enter their comments:

```
import React, { useState } from 'react';



function MyForm() {

  // ... (other state variables)

  const [comments, setComments] =
useState('');



  const handleChange = (event) => {

    // ... (handling for other fields)



    if (event.target.name === 'comments') {

      setComments(event.target.value);

    }

  };



  // ... (handleSubmit function)
```

```
return (
```

In this code:

- We initialize the `comments` state variable to an empty string using `useState('')`.

- The `handleChange` function handles changes to the textarea element. We update the `comments` state variable with the text entered by the user using `setComments(event.target.value)`.

- The `value` attribute of the textarea element is bound to the `comments` state variable.

File Input Elements

File input elements allow users to upload files. Handling file uploads in React requires a slightly different approach compared to other form elements.

Instead of binding the file input element's value to a state variable, you typically access the selected file from the event object in the event handler.

Let's add a file input element to our form to allow the user to upload their profile picture:

```
import React, { useState } from 'react';
```

```
function MyForm() {

   // ... (other state variables)

   const [profilePicture, setProfilePicture]
= useState(null);


   const handleChange = (event) => {

     // ... (handling for other fields)


     if (event.target.name ===
'profilePicture') {

setProfilePicture(event.target.files[0]);

     }

   };


   // ... (handleSubmit function)


   return (
```

In this code:

- We initialize the `profilePicture` state variable to `null` using `useState(null)`.

- The `handleChange` function handles changes to the file input element. We access the selected file using `event.target.files[0]` and update the `profilePicture` state variable.

- When the user selects a file, the `profilePicture` state variable will contain a `File` object representing the selected file. You can then send this file to your back-end API for processing.

Data Validation

Data validation is an essential aspect of form handling. It ensures that the data entered by the user meets certain criteria, such as required fields, data types, and format.

React doesn't provide built-in data validation mechanisms, but you can easily implement data validation using JavaScript's built-in validation features or third-party libraries like `validator`.

Let's add some basic data validation to our form. We'll make the name and email fields required and validate the email format:

```
import React, { useState } from 'react';

import validator from 'validator';


function MyForm() {

  // ... (other state variables)

  const [errors, setErrors] = useState({});
```

```
const handleChange = (event) => {

  // ... (handling for other fields)


  setErrors({ ...errors,
[event.target.name]: '' }); // Clear error
for the field

};


const handleSubmit = (event) => {

  event.preventDefault();


  const newErrors = {};


  if (name.trim() === '') {

    newErrors.name = 'Name is required';

  }


  if (email.trim() === '') {

    newErrors.email = 'Email is required';
```

```
    } else if (!validator.isEmail(email)) {

      newErrors.email = 'Invalid email
format';

    }


    if (Object.keys(newErrors).length > 0) {

      setErrors(newErrors);

      return;

    }


    // TODO: Send form data to the back-end

  };


  return (
```

In this code:

- We import the `validator` library.

- We initialize the `errors` state variable to an empty object using `useState({})`. This object will store validation errors for each field.

- The `handleChange` function now clears the error for the field that has changed.

- The `handleSubmit` function performs the data validation. We create a `newErrors` object to store the validation errors.

- We check if the name and email fields are empty or if the email format is invalid. If any validation errors are found, we update the `errors` state variable with the `newErrors` object and prevent the form submission.

- We conditionally render error messages next to each field based on the `errors` state.

Submitting Form Data to the Back-end

Once the form data has been validated, you can submit it to your back-end API for processing. You can use Axios or the built-in `fetch` API to make a POST request to your API endpoint, passing the form data as the request body.

Let's update the `handleSubmit` function to send the form data to the back-end:

```
import React, { useState } from 'react';

import validator from 'validator';

import axios from 'axios';


function MyForm() {

  // ... (other state variables and
functions)
```

```javascript
const handleSubmit = async (event) => {

    event.preventDefault();


    // ... (data validation)


    try {

        const response = await
axios.post('/api/users', {

            name: name,

            email: email,

            newsletter: newsletter,

            color: color,

            comments: comments,

            profilePicture: profilePicture,

        });


        console.log('Form submitted
successfully:', response.data);

    } catch (error) {
```

```
      console.error('Error submitting
form:', error);

    }

  };



  // ... (rest of the component)

}



export default MyForm;
```

In this code:

- We import the `axios` library.

- Inside the `handleSubmit` function, after the data validation, we make a POST request to the `/api/users` endpoint using `axios.post()`. We pass the form data as an object in the request body.

- If the request is successful, we log the response data to the console.

- If an error occurs, we log the error to the console.

Form Libraries and Frameworks

While React provides the foundation for building forms, there are various third-party libraries and frameworks that can simplify and enhance form handling in React applications. These libraries offer features such as form validation, form state management, and form styling.

Some popular form libraries and frameworks for React include:

- **Formik:** A popular form library that provides a declarative way to define forms, handle form state, and perform form validation.

- **React Hook Form:** A performance-focused form library that uses React Hooks to manage form state and validation.

- **Redux Form:** A library that integrates forms with Redux for state management.

These libraries can save you time and effort by providing pre-built components and functionalities for handling common form-related tasks.

Forms are the gateways through which users interact with your web applications, providing information, making choices, and initiating actions. React's controlled component approach, coupled with techniques for handling form submission, managing multiple fields, data validation, and back-end integration, empowers you to create forms that are both user-friendly and efficient. As you continue your React journey, remember to leverage these techniques and explore the vast ecosystem of form libraries and frameworks to streamline your form development process and build interactive and engaging user experiences.

Chapter Fourteen: Styling Your React Application

In the previous chapters, we've covered the essentials of building dynamic and interactive React applications, from managing state and handling events to fetching data from APIs and routing between different views. We've focused on the functionality and logic of our applications, but what about their appearance? In this chapter, we'll turn our attention to styling, the art of making our React applications visually appealing and user-friendly. We'll explore various techniques for styling React components, from inline styles and CSS Modules to the powerful paradigm of CSS-in-JS using styled-components. We'll learn how to add a touch of style and personality to our applications, transforming them from functional skeletons into visually engaging and delightful experiences for our users.

Inline Styles: The Direct Approach

The most straightforward way to style React components is by using inline styles. Inline styles involve applying styles directly to an element using the `style` attribute in JSX. The `style` attribute takes an object where the keys are CSS property names in camelCase and the values are CSS property values.

Let's illustrate inline styles with an example. Suppose we want to style a heading to have a red color and a font size of 24 pixels:

```
import React from 'react';


function MyComponent() {

  return (
```

```
    <h1 style={{ color: 'red', fontSize:
'24px' }}>

        Hello, React!

    </h1>

  );

}



export default MyComponent;
```

In this code, we apply the inline styles `color: 'red'` and `fontSize: '24px'` to the `<h1>` element using the `style` attribute.

While inline styles are convenient for simple styling, they have a few drawbacks:

- **Limited Reusability:** Inline styles are applied directly to individual elements, making it difficult to reuse styles across multiple elements or components.

- **No Cascading:** Inline styles don't cascade, meaning that styles applied to parent elements don't automatically apply to child elements.

- **Difficult to Maintain:** As your application grows, managing inline styles can become cumbersome and difficult to maintain, especially when dealing with complex styling rules.

CSS Classes: The Traditional Approach

A more maintainable approach to styling React components is by using CSS classes. CSS classes allow you to define styles in separate CSS files and apply them to multiple elements by assigning the same class name to those elements.

Let's create a separate CSS file named MyComponent.css and add the following styles:

```css
.my-heading {

  color: red;

  font-size: 24px;

}
```

Now, we can import this CSS file into our React component and apply the my-heading class to the <h1> element:

```jsx
import React from 'react';

import './MyComponent.css';


function MyComponent() {

  return (

    <h1 className="my-heading">
```

```
      Hello, React!

    </h1>

  );

}



export default MyComponent;
```

Using CSS classes offers several advantages over inline styles:

- **Reusability:** CSS classes can be applied to multiple elements, promoting style reusability and consistency across your application.

- **Cascading:** CSS styles cascade, meaning that styles applied to parent elements automatically apply to child elements, unless overridden by more specific styles.

- **Maintainability:** Separating styles into dedicated CSS files makes it easier to manage and maintain your application's styling as it grows.

CSS Modules: Encapsulation and Namespacing

While CSS classes provide a more maintainable approach to styling, they can still lead to naming conflicts, especially in large projects where multiple developers might be working on different components. CSS Modules address this issue by providing encapsulation and namespacing for your CSS styles.

CSS Modules are a build-time feature that transforms your CSS files into modules with unique class names. This ensures that the class names you define in your CSS files are scoped to the component where they are imported, preventing naming conflicts.

Let's create a CSS Module named `MyComponent.module.css` and add the following styles:

```css
.heading {

  color: red;

  font-size: 24px;

}
```

Now, we can import this CSS Module into our React component and access the generated class names:

```jsx
import React from 'react';

import styles from
'./MyComponent.module.css';


function MyComponent() {

  return (

    <h1 className={styles.heading}>
```

```
      Hello, React!

   </h1>

 );

}
```

```
export default MyComponent;
```

In this code:

- We import the CSS Module as `styles`.

- The imported `styles` object contains the generated class names, in this case, `styles.heading`.

- We apply the generated class name to the `<h1>` element.

CSS Modules offer several benefits:

- **Encapsulation:** CSS styles are scoped to the component where they are imported, preventing naming conflicts.

- **Namespacing:** Generated class names are unique, ensuring that styles don't accidentally leak to other components.

- **Improved Maintainability:** CSS Modules make it easier to manage and maintain styles, as each component has its dedicated CSS module.

CSS-in-JS: The Power of JavaScript

CSS-in-JS is a paradigm that allows you to write CSS styles using JavaScript. This approach brings the power and flexibility of JavaScript to CSS, enabling you to use variables, functions, conditional logic, and other JavaScript features to create dynamic and expressive styles.

One popular CSS-in-JS library is styled-components. Styled-components allow you to create reusable, encapsulated, and themeable components that have their styles defined using JavaScript template literals.

Let's illustrate styled-components with an example. Suppose we want to create a reusable button component with different styles for primary and secondary buttons:

```
import styled from 'styled-components';


const Button = styled.button`

    padding: 10px 20px;

    border: none;

    border-radius: 5px;

    font-size: 16px;

    cursor: pointer;


    &.primary {

        background-color: #007bff;
```

```
    color: #fff;

  }


  &.secondary {

    background-color: #6c757d;

    color: #fff;

  }
`;


function MyComponent() {

  return (

    <div>

      <Button className="primary">Primary
Button</Button>

      <Button
className="secondary">Secondary
Button</Button>

    </div>

  );

}
```

```
export default MyComponent;
```

In this code:

- We import the `styled` object from styled-components.

- We create a styled component named `Button` using `styled.button`.

- We define the base styles for the button within the template literal.

- We define styles for primary and secondary buttons using CSS selectors within the template literal.

- We render two instances of the `Button` component, one with the `primary` class and one with the `secondary` class.

Styled-components offer several benefits:

- **Component-Based Styling:** Styles are encapsulated within components, promoting reusability and maintainability.

- **Dynamic Styling:** You can use JavaScript variables, functions, and conditional logic to create dynamic styles based on props, state, or other factors.

- **Themeability:** Styled-components support theming, allowing you to easily switch between different stylesheets for your application.

- **Automatic Vendor Prefixing:** Styled-components automatically add vendor prefixes to your styles, ensuring cross-browser compatibility.

Other CSS-in-JS Libraries

Besides styled-components, there are other popular CSS-in-JS libraries available, each with its strengths and weaknesses:

- **Emotion:** A high-performance CSS-in-JS library that offers both a compile-time and a runtime approach to styling.

- **JSS:** A CSS-in-JS library that focuses on low-level CSS object manipulation and supports server-side rendering.

- **Glamorous:** A CSS-in-JS library that emphasizes component-based styling and provides a declarative API.

The choice of a CSS-in-JS library depends on your project's requirements, your team's preferences, and your personal coding style.

Choosing the Right Styling Approach

The best approach to styling your React application depends on various factors, including the size and complexity of your project, your team's experience, and your personal preferences.

Here are some general guidelines:

- **Inline Styles:** Suitable for simple styling that doesn't need to be reused.

- **CSS Classes:** A good choice for most applications, especially when combined with CSS Modules for encapsulation and namespacing.

- **CSS-in-JS:** A powerful option for dynamic styling, themeability, and component-based styling, but it might introduce some overhead and complexity.

Styling Best Practices

Regardless of the styling approach you choose, there are some general best practices to follow:

- **Keep Styles Organized:** Organize your styles into separate files or modules based on components or features.

- **Use Meaningful Names:** Choose meaningful and descriptive names for your CSS classes, selectors, and variables.

- **Avoid Global Styles:** Minimize the use of global styles to prevent unintended side effects and improve maintainability.

- **Use a CSS Preprocessor:** Consider using a CSS preprocessor like Sass or Less to enhance your CSS workflow with features like variables, nesting, and mixins.

- **Test Your Styles:** Test your styles across different browsers and devices to ensure cross-browser compatibility and responsiveness.

Styling is an integral part of crafting user-friendly and visually appealing React applications. By exploring various styling techniques, from inline styles to CSS-in-JS, you gain a diverse toolkit for adding a touch of style and personality to your applications. Whether you prefer the traditional approach of CSS classes or the flexibility of CSS-in-JS, remember to choose the approach that best suits your project's needs and your team's workflow. As you continue your React journey, embrace the power of styling to transform your functional applications into engaging and delightful experiences for your users.

Chapter Fifteen: Authenticating Users with JWT

In the ever-evolving landscape of web development, security stands as a paramount concern. As we craft applications that handle sensitive user data and facilitate interactions between users, ensuring the authenticity and authorization of users becomes crucial. This chapter delves into the realm of user authentication, a vital aspect of building secure and trustworthy MERN stack applications. We'll explore the concept of JSON Web Tokens (JWT), a powerful and widely adopted standard for securely transmitting information between parties. We'll learn how to implement user authentication using JWT in our MERN stack applications, enabling us to verify user identities and protect sensitive data from unauthorized access.

User Authentication: Verifying Identities

User authentication is the process of verifying the identity of a user who is attempting to access a system or application. It involves confirming that the user is indeed who they claim to be, preventing unauthorized individuals from gaining access to sensitive data or performing actions they are not permitted to do.

Think of user authentication as a bouncer at a nightclub. The bouncer's job is to check IDs and ensure that only those who meet the entry requirements are allowed in. Similarly, user authentication mechanisms in web applications act as gatekeepers, verifying user credentials and granting access only to authorized users.

Traditional Authentication Methods

Traditional web applications often rely on session-based authentication. In this approach, when a user logs in, the server creates a session for the user and stores session data on the server-side. The server then sends a unique session ID to the client,

211

typically stored in a cookie. With each subsequent request, the client sends the session ID back to the server, allowing the server to identify the user and retrieve their session data.

While session-based authentication is a common approach, it has some limitations:

- **Scalability:** Session data is stored on the server-side, which can become a bottleneck as the number of users and sessions increases.

- **Statefulness:** Session-based authentication requires the server to maintain state, meaning the server needs to keep track of all active sessions. This can add complexity to the server-side logic.

- **Cross-Domain Issues:** Cookies used to store session IDs can face cross-domain issues, especially when dealing with APIs that reside on different domains.

JSON Web Token (JWT): A Stateless Solution

JSON Web Token (JWT) offers a stateless and more scalable approach to user authentication. JWT is an open standard (RFC 7519) that defines a compact and self-contained way for securely transmitting information between parties as a JSON object.

A JWT consists of three parts:

- **Header:** The header typically specifies the type of the token (JWT) and the algorithm used to sign the token.

- **Payload:** The payload contains the claims or information about the user, such as their user ID, email address, or roles.

- **Signature:** The signature is created by signing the header and payload with a secret key. The signature ensures the integrity and authenticity of the token, preventing tampering.

The three parts of the JWT are encoded using Base64Url and separated by dots, resulting in a string that looks like this:

eyJhbGciOiJIUzI1NiIsInR5cCI6IkpXVCJ9.eyJzdWIiOiIxMjM0N TY3ODkwIiwibmFtZSI6IkpvaG4gRG9lIiwiaWF0IjoxNTE2MjM 5MDIyfQ.SflKxwRJSMeKKF2QT4fwpMeJf36POk6yJV_adQssw 5c

The Benefits of JWT

JWT offers several benefits over traditional session-based authentication:

- **Statelessness:** JWTs are self-contained, meaning all the information about the user is embedded within the token itself. The server doesn't need to maintain any session data, making JWT a stateless authentication mechanism.

- **Scalability:** Since the server doesn't need to store session data, JWT-based authentication is highly scalable.

- **Security:** JWTs are signed with a secret key, ensuring the integrity and authenticity of the token.

- **Cross-Domain Compatibility:** JWTs can be easily transmitted across different domains without facing cookie-related issues.

Implementing JWT Authentication in MERN

Let's implement JWT authentication in our MERN stack application. We'll start by installing the necessary dependencies. Open your terminal or command prompt, navigate to the root directory of your server project, and run the following command:

```
npm install jsonwebtoken bcryptjs
```

This command will install the jsonwebtoken and bcryptjs libraries. jsonwebtoken is used to create and verify JWTs, while bcryptjs is used to hash passwords securely.

User Registration

Let's create a route for user registration. This route will handle creating new user accounts in our database. Open your index.js file on the server-side and add the following code:

```
const express = require('express');

const bcrypt = require('bcryptjs');

const jwt = require('jsonwebtoken');

const User = require('./models/User');



const router = express.Router();



// User registration

router.post('/register', async (req, res) =>
{
  try {
```

```javascript
    const { name, email, password } =
req.body;


    // Check if user already exists

    let user = await User.findOne({ email
});

    if (user) {

        return res.status(400).json({ msg:
'User already exists' });

    }


    user = new User({

        name,

        email,

        password,

    });


    // Hash password

    const salt = await bcrypt.genSalt(10);

    user.password = await
bcrypt.hash(password, salt);
```

```
await user.save();


// Create JWT payload

const payload = {

  user: {

    id: user.id,

  },

};


// Sign JWT

jwt.sign(

  payload,

  'your-secret-key', // Replace with
your secret key

  { expiresIn: 3600 }, // Token expires
in 1 hour

  (err, token) => {

    if (err) throw err;

    res.json({ token });

  }
```

```
    );

  } catch (err) {

    console.error(err.message);

    res.status(500).send('Server Error');

  }

});


module.exports = router;
```

In this code:

- We import the bcryptjs and jsonwebtoken libraries.

- We define a route for POST requests to /register.

- Inside the route handler:

- We check if a user with the given email already exists. If so, we return an error response.

- We create a new user object using the data received in the request body.

- We hash the user's password using bcryptjs.

- We save the new user to the database.

- We create a JWT payload containing the user's ID.

- We sign the JWT using our secret key and set an expiration time of 1 hour.

- We send the JWT as a response to the client.

User Login

Now, let's create a route for user login. This route will handle authenticating users and issuing JWTs upon successful login. Add the following code to your `index.js` file:

```
// ... (other code)


// User login

router.post('/login', async (req, res) => {

  try {

    const { email, password } = req.body;



    // Check if user exists

    let user = await User.findOne({ email
});

    if (!user) {

      return res.status(400).json({ msg:
'Invalid Credentials' });

    }
```

```
// Compare password

const isMatch = await
bcrypt.compare(password, user.password);

if (!isMatch) {

    return res.status(400).json({ msg:
'Invalid Credentials' });

}


// Create JWT payload

const payload = {

  user: {

    id: user.id,

  },

};


// Sign JWT

jwt.sign(

  payload,

    'your-secret-key', // Replace with
your secret key
```

```
      { expiresIn: 3600 }, // Token expires
in 1 hour

      (err, token) => {

        if (err) throw err;

        res.json({ token });

      }

    );

  } catch (err) {

    console.error(err.message);

    res.status(500).send('Server Error');

  }

});


module.exports = router;
```

In this code:

- We define a route for POST requests to /login.

- Inside the route handler:

- We check if a user with the given email exists. If not, we return an error response.

- We compare the entered password with the hashed password stored in the database using `bcryptjs.compare()`. If the passwords don't match, we return an error response.

- We create a JWT payload containing the user's ID.

- We sign the JWT using our secret key and set an expiration time of 1 hour.

- We send the JWT as a response to the client.

Protecting Routes

Now that we have our user registration and login routes set up, let's protect a route using JWT authentication. This means that only authenticated users with a valid JWT will be able to access the protected route.

Let's create a simple route that returns a message for authenticated users. Add the following code to your `index.js` file:

```
// ... (other code)



// Protected route

router.get('/protected', auth, async (req,
res) => {

   try {

      res.json({ msg: 'Welcome, authenticated
user!' });

   } catch (err) {
```

```
    console.error(err.message);

    res.status(500).send('Server Error');

  }

});


// Middleware function to authenticate
requests

function auth(req, res, next) {

  // Get token from header

  const token = req.header('x-auth-token');


  // Check if not token

  if (!token) {

    return res.status(401).json({ msg: 'No
token, authorization denied' });

  }


  try {

    // Verify token
```

```
    const decoded = jwt.verify(token, 'your-
secret-key'); // Replace with your secret
key


    // Add user from payload to request
object

    req.user = decoded.user;

    next();

  } catch (err) {

    res.status(401).json({ msg: 'Token is
not valid' });

  }

}


module.exports = router;
```

In this code:

- We define a route for GET requests to /protected.

- We use a middleware function auth to authenticate requests to this route.

- Inside the auth middleware:

- We get the JWT from the `x-auth-token` header of the request.

- We check if a token is provided. If not, we return an error response.

- We verify the JWT using our secret key. If the token is invalid or expired, an error will be thrown.

- We add the user object from the JWT payload to the request object (`req.user`).

- We call `next()` to pass control to the next middleware or route handler.

- If the JWT is valid, the route handler will be executed, and the message "Welcome, authenticated user!" will be returned to the client.

Accessing User Information in Protected Routes

In protected routes, you can access information about the authenticated user from the `req.user` object. This object contains the user's ID and any other claims that were included in the JWT payload.

You can use this information to personalize the response, retrieve user-specific data from the database, or perform other actions that require knowledge of the authenticated user's identity.

Logout

Logout in JWT-based authentication is typically handled on the client-side. When the user logs out, the client simply removes the JWT from local storage or cookies. Since JWTs are stateless, there's no need to explicitly invalidate the token on the server-side.

Token Refresh

JWTs have an expiration time, after which they become invalid. To provide a seamless user experience, you might want to implement token refresh mechanisms.

One approach is to issue a refresh token along with the access token. The refresh token has a longer expiration time than the access token. When the access token expires, the client can use the refresh token to request a new access token from the server.

JWT Best Practices

Here are some best practices for using JWT in your applications:

- **Store Secret Key Securely:** Never store your secret key in your client-side code or commit it to version control. Use environment variables or other secure mechanisms to store your secret key.

- **Use HTTPS:** Always use HTTPS to transmit JWTs to prevent eavesdropping and man-in-the-middle attacks.

- **Set Appropriate Expiration Times:** Choose appropriate expiration times for your access and refresh tokens based on your application's security requirements and user experience considerations.

- **Use a Strong Algorithm:** Use a strong cryptographic algorithm to sign your JWTs, such as HS256 or RS256.

- **Consider Token Blacklisting:** In scenarios where you need to revoke tokens before their expiration time, implement token blacklisting mechanisms.

User authentication is a critical aspect of building secure and trustworthy web applications. JWT provides a stateless, scalable, and secure approach to user authentication, addressing many of the limitations of traditional session-based authentication. By mastering the concepts of JWT and implementing JWT authentication in our MERN stack applications, we can ensure the authenticity and authorization of our users, safeguarding sensitive data and building robust and reliable applications. As you continue your journey in web development, remember that user authentication is an ongoing process that requires careful consideration, implementation, and ongoing maintenance to protect your users and your applications.

Chapter Sixteen: Authorization and Access Control

In the previous chapter, we explored the world of user authentication using JWT (JSON Web Token), learning how to verify user identities and protect sensitive routes from unauthorized access. Authentication lays the foundation for security, but it's only the first step. Once we know who the user is, we need to determine what they are allowed to do. This is where authorization and access control come into play. Authorization goes beyond mere identity verification and focuses on granting or denying access to specific resources or actions based on the user's roles, permissions, or other attributes. In this chapter, we'll delve into the concepts of authorization and access control, exploring various techniques for implementing them in our MERN stack applications, ensuring that users can only perform actions they are authorized to perform.

Authorization: Granting Access Based on Roles and Permissions

Authorization is the process of determining whether a user has the necessary permissions to access a particular resource or perform a specific action. It builds upon authentication by adding a layer of control that governs what authenticated users are allowed to do within the application.

Think of authorization as a security guard at a concert. While the ticket checker at the entrance (authentication) verifies that you have a valid ticket, the security guard inside the venue (authorization) determines which areas you can access based on your ticket type. You might have a general admission ticket that grants you access to certain areas, while a VIP ticket might grant you access to exclusive areas backstage.

In web applications, authorization is often based on roles and permissions.

- **Roles:** Roles represent groups of users with similar permissions. For example, you might have roles like "admin," "editor," and "viewer," each with different levels of access.

- **Permissions:** Permissions are specific actions that a user is allowed to perform. For example, a user with the "edit" permission might be allowed to edit content, while a user with the "view" permission can only view content.

Implementing Role-Based Access Control (RBAC)

Role-Based Access Control (RBAC) is a widely used authorization model that grants access to resources based on the roles assigned to users. In RBAC, you define roles and assign permissions to those roles. Users are then assigned to one or more roles, inheriting the permissions associated with those roles.

Let's illustrate RBAC with an example. Suppose we have a blog application with the following roles and permissions:

Role	Permissions
Admin	Create, Read, Update, Delete all posts; Manage users
Editor	Create, Read, Update, Delete their own posts; Read other posts
Viewer	Read all posts

In this scenario:

- An admin has the highest level of access, being able to perform all actions on all posts and manage users.

- An editor can create, read, update, and delete their own posts, but they can only read posts created by other users.

- A viewer has the lowest level of access, being able to only read posts.

Implementing Authorization in MERN

Let's implement RBAC in our MERN stack application. We'll start by adding a `role` field to our `User` model on the server-side. Open your `User.js` file in the `models` directory and modify the schema as follows:

```
const mongoose = require('mongoose');


const UserSchema = new mongoose.Schema({
  name: {
    type: String,
    required: true,
  },
  email: {
    type: String,
    required: true,
    unique: true,
  },
  password: {
    type: String,
    required: true,
```

```
  },

  role: {

    type: String,

    enum: ['admin', 'editor', 'viewer'],

    default: 'viewer',

  },

});
```

```
module.exports = mongoose.model('User',
UserSchema);
```

In this code:

- We add a role field to the UserSchema.

- We use the enum validator to ensure that the role field can only take one of three values: "admin," "editor," or "viewer."

- We set the default role to "viewer."

Authorizing Requests Based on Roles

Now, let's modify our protected route to check the user's role and grant or deny access accordingly. Open your index.js file on the server-side and modify the protected route as follows:

```javascript
// ... (other code)

// Protected route

router.get('/protected', auth, async (req,
res) => {

  try {

    // Check if user is an admin

    if (req.user.role === 'admin') {

      return res.json({ msg: 'Welcome, admin
user!' });

    }


    // Check if user is an editor

    if (req.user.role === 'editor') {

      return res.json({ msg: 'Welcome,
editor user!' });

    }


    // Default message for viewers

    res.json({ msg: 'Welcome, viewer user!'
});
```

```
  } catch (err) {

    console.error(err.message);

    res.status(500).send('Server Error');

  }

});



// ... (auth middleware)
```

In this code:

- We check the user's role from the `req.user` object, which is populated by the `auth` middleware.

- We return different messages based on the user's role.

Custom Middleware for Authorization

We can create custom middleware functions to handle authorization logic for specific routes or actions. This allows us to centralize authorization logic and reuse it across different routes.

Let's create a middleware function to check if the user is an admin. Add the following code to your `index.js` file:

```
// ... (other code)
```

```javascript
// Middleware function to check if user is
an admin

function isAdmin(req, res, next) {

  // Check if user is authenticated

  if (!req.user) {

    return res.status(401).json({ msg: 'No
token, authorization denied' });

  }


  // Check if user is an admin

  if (req.user.role !== 'admin') {

    return res.status(403).json({ msg:
'Forbidden' });

  }


  next();

}


// Protected route for admins only

router.get('/admin', auth, isAdmin, async
(req, res) => {

  try {
```

```
      res.json({ msg: 'Welcome, admin user!'
});

  } catch (err) {

    console.error(err.message);

    res.status(500).send('Server Error');

  }

});



// ... (other code)
```

In this code:

- We define a middleware function isAdmin that checks if the user is an admin.

- We use this middleware in the protected route /admin, along with the auth middleware.

- If the user is not an admin, the isAdmin middleware will return a 403 (Forbidden) error response.

Permission-Based Access Control (PBAC)

Permission-Based Access Control (PBAC) is a more fine-grained authorization model that grants access to resources based on specific permissions assigned to users. In PBAC, you define permissions and assign them directly to users or roles. Users can then access resources or perform actions only if they have the required permissions.

PBAC offers more flexibility than RBAC, allowing you to define very specific permissions for different users or roles. However, it can also be more complex to manage, as you need to keep track of individual permissions.

Implementing PBAC in MERN

To implement PBAC in our MERN stack application, we can modify our `User` model to store an array of permissions. We can then create middleware functions to check if the user has the required permissions for specific routes or actions.

For example, we could modify our `User` model schema as follows:

```
const mongoose = require('mongoose');


const UserSchema = new mongoose.Schema({

  // ... (other fields)


  permissions: [String],

});



module.exports = mongoose.model('User',
UserSchema);
```

In this schema, the permissions field is an array of strings, where each string represents a permission. We can then create a middleware function to check if the user has a specific permission:

```
function hasPermission(permission) {

  return function (req, res, next) {

    // Check if user is authenticated

    if (!req.user) {

      return res.status(401).json({ msg: 'No
token, authorization denied' });

    }


    // Check if user has the required
permission

    if
(!req.user.permissions.includes(permission))
{

      return res.status(403).json({ msg:
'Forbidden' });

    }


    next();
```

```
    };

}
```

This middleware function takes a permission as an argument and returns a middleware function that checks if the user has that permission. We can then use this middleware in our protected routes:

```
router.get('/edit-post', auth,
hasPermission('edit-post'), async (req, res)
=> {

    // ... route handler logic

});
```

In this route, the `hasPermission('edit-post')` middleware will check if the authenticated user has the `edit-post` permission before allowing them to access the route.

Access Control Lists (ACLs)

Access Control Lists (ACLs) are another authorization mechanism that allows you to define permissions for specific resources. In ACLs, you associate a list of permissions with each resource. Each entry in the ACL specifies a user or role and the permissions they have for that resource.

ACLs provide a granular way to control access to individual resources. However, they can be more complex to manage than RBAC or PBAC, as you need to maintain ACLs for each resource.

Attribute-Based Access Control (ABAC)

Attribute-Based Access Control (ABAC) is a more dynamic and flexible authorization model that grants access based on attributes of the user, resource, and environment. In ABAC, you define policies that specify the conditions under which access is granted or denied. These policies can be based on any attribute, such as user role, location, time of day, or device type.

ABAC offers a high level of flexibility and granularity, allowing you to define very specific access control rules. However, it can also be more complex to implement and manage.

Best Practices for Authorization

Here are some best practices for implementing authorization in your MERN stack applications:

- **Principle of Least Privilege:** Grant users only the permissions they need to perform their tasks. Avoid granting excessive permissions.

- **Centralize Authorization Logic:** Use middleware functions or other mechanisms to centralize authorization logic and avoid repeating it in multiple routes.

- **Use a Consistent Authorization Model:** Choose an authorization model (RBAC, PBAC, ACLs, or ABAC) that best suits your application's requirements and stick to it consistently.

- **Test Authorization Thoroughly:** Test your authorization logic thoroughly to ensure that users can access only the resources they are authorized to access.

- **Consider Security Frameworks:** Explore security frameworks like OAuth 2.0 and OpenID Connect for more advanced authorization scenarios.

Authorization and access control are essential aspects of building secure and trustworthy MERN stack applications. By implementing authorization mechanisms, we can ensure that users can only perform actions they are permitted to do, protecting sensitive data and maintaining the integrity of our applications. Whether you choose role-based access control, permission-based access control, or more advanced authorization models, remember to apply the principle of least privilege, centralize authorization logic, and test your authorization mechanisms thoroughly.

Chapter Seventeen: Deploying Your MERN Stack Application

Up to this point, we've delved deep into the intricacies of building MERN stack applications. We've learned how to craft robust back-ends using Node.js, Express.js, and MongoDB, as well as dynamic and interactive front-ends using React.js. We've explored concepts like state management, data fetching, routing, authentication, and authorization, equipping ourselves with a comprehensive set of tools for building full-fledged web applications. However, our applications have been confined to our local development environments, accessible only to us. In this chapter, we'll take the crucial step of deploying our MERN stack applications, making them accessible to the world via the internet. We'll explore various deployment options, learn about popular cloud platforms, and walk through the process of deploying a MERN application step-by-step, bringing our creations to life and sharing them with the world.

Deployment: Bridging the Gap Between Development and Production

Deployment is the process of making your application accessible to users over the internet. It involves taking your application code, along with its dependencies and configurations, and placing it on a server that's connected to the internet, allowing users to access it from their web browsers.

Deployment is a critical step in the application development lifecycle, as it bridges the gap between development and production. While you've been developing your application locally, deployment makes it available to real users, allowing them to interact with and benefit from your creation.

Deployment Options: A Spectrum of Choices

There are various deployment options available, each with its advantages and considerations. The choice of a deployment option depends on factors such as the complexity of your application, your budget, your technical expertise, and your scalability requirements.

Let's explore some popular deployment options:

Shared Hosting: A Budget-Friendly Option

Shared hosting is a cost-effective deployment option where multiple websites share the same server resources. It's a good choice for small websites or applications with low traffic, as it offers a low barrier to entry and requires minimal technical expertise.

However, shared hosting has limitations in terms of performance, customization, and security. Since multiple websites share the same server resources, your application's performance might be affected by other websites on the same server. Additionally, shared hosting environments often have limited customization options and might not provide the level of security required for applications handling sensitive data.

Virtual Private Server (VPS): Greater Control and Flexibility

A Virtual Private Server (VPS) offers more control and flexibility compared to shared hosting. A VPS is a virtualized server that runs on a physical server, sharing the physical server's resources with other VPSs. However, each VPS has its own operating system and resources, providing greater isolation and customization options.

VPS hosting provides a good balance between cost and performance, offering more resources and flexibility than shared hosting while remaining more affordable than dedicated servers. It's suitable for applications with moderate traffic or specific configuration requirements.

Dedicated Server: Unrivaled Performance and Security

A dedicated server provides the highest level of performance, security, and customization. With a dedicated server, you have exclusive access to the server's resources, ensuring that your application's performance is not affected by other websites or applications.

Dedicated servers are the most expensive hosting option, but they offer unparalleled performance, security, and control, making them suitable for high-traffic applications or those handling sensitive data.

Cloud Hosting: Scalability and Flexibility on Demand

Cloud hosting has emerged as a popular and flexible deployment option in recent years. Cloud hosting providers offer a wide range of services, including virtual servers, databases, storage, and more, all delivered over the internet.

Cloud hosting offers several benefits:

- **Scalability:** Cloud platforms allow you to easily scale your application's resources up or down based on demand, ensuring that your application can handle traffic spikes without performance degradation.

- **Flexibility:** Cloud platforms offer a wide range of services and configurations, allowing you to choose the best options for your application's needs.

- **Cost-Effectiveness:** Cloud hosting can be cost-effective, as you only pay for the resources you use.

- **Reliability:** Cloud platforms are designed for high availability and redundancy, ensuring that your application is always accessible.

Popular Cloud Platforms: AWS, Azure, and Google Cloud

Several major cloud platforms dominate the market, each offering a comprehensive suite of services for deploying and managing applications.

Amazon Web Services (AWS)

Amazon Web Services (AWS) is the world's largest and most comprehensive cloud platform, offering a vast array of services, including computing, storage, databases, networking, analytics, and more.

AWS provides services like:

- **EC2 (Elastic Compute Cloud):** Virtual servers that you can customize to meet your application's needs.

- **S3 (Simple Storage Service):** Object storage for storing files, images, videos, and other data.

- **RDS (Relational Database Service):** Managed relational databases, such as MySQL, PostgreSQL, and SQL Server.

- **Lambda:** Serverless computing platform for running code without provisioning or managing servers.

Microsoft Azure

Microsoft Azure is another major cloud platform that offers a wide range of services comparable to AWS. Azure is particularly popular among enterprises that already use Microsoft products and services.

Azure provides services like:

- **Virtual Machines:** Virtual servers similar to AWS EC2.

- **Azure Blob Storage:** Object storage similar to AWS S3.

- **Azure SQL Database:** Managed SQL Server databases.

- **Azure Functions:** Serverless computing platform similar to AWS Lambda.

Google Cloud Platform (GCP)

Google Cloud Platform (GCP) is Google's cloud computing platform, offering a suite of services for computing, storage, databases, networking, and more. GCP is known for its strong focus on data analytics and machine learning.

GCP provides services like:

- **Compute Engine:** Virtual servers similar to AWS EC2.

- **Cloud Storage:** Object storage similar to AWS S3.

- **Cloud SQL:** Managed MySQL, PostgreSQL, and SQL Server databases.

- **Cloud Functions:** Serverless computing platform similar to AWS Lambda.

Deploying a MERN Application to Heroku

For this demonstration, we'll deploy a simple MERN application to Heroku, a popular cloud platform that makes it easy to deploy and manage web applications. Heroku offers a free tier that's suitable for small projects or prototypes.

Prerequisites

Before we begin, ensure that you have the following prerequisites:

- **Heroku Account:** Create a free Heroku account at https://www.heroku.com.

- **Heroku CLI:** Install the Heroku Command Line Interface (CLI) from https://devcenter.heroku.com/articles/heroku-cli.

- **Git:** Ensure that you have Git installed on your computer.

Project Setup

Let's start by creating a simple MERN application. We'll use Create React App to generate a basic React front-end and Express.js for the back-end.

Open your terminal or command prompt and create a new directory for your project:

```
mkdir my-mern-app

cd my-mern-app
```

Now, create the React front-end using Create React App:

```
npx create-react-app client
```

This command will create a new directory named client and generate a basic React application within it.

Next, create the Express.js back-end. Create a new directory named server and navigate to it:

```
mkdir server

cd server
```

Initialize a new Node.js project:

```
npm init -y
```

Install the necessary dependencies:

```
npm install express cors
```

We'll use the cors middleware to enable cross-origin requests, allowing our front-end to communicate with our back-end.

Create a file named index.js within the server directory and add the following code:

```
const express = require('express');
```

```javascript
const cors = require('cors');


const app = express();


// Enable CORS

app.use(cors());


// Define a simple API endpoint

app.get('/api/message', (req, res) => {

   res.json({ message: 'Hello from the
server!' });

});


const PORT = process.env.PORT || 5000;


app.listen(PORT, () => console.log(`Server
running on port ${PORT}`));
```

This code defines a simple Express.js server that listens on port 5000 (or the port specified by the PORT environment variable) and responds to GET requests to the /api/message endpoint with a JSON object containing a message.

Now, let's modify our React front-end to fetch this message from the back-end. Open the `App.js` file within the `client` directory and replace its contents with the following code:

```
import React, { useState, useEffect } from
'react';

import axios from 'axios';


function App() {

  const [message, setMessage] =
useState('');



  useEffect(() => {

    const fetchMessage = async () => {

      try {

        const response = await
axios.get('/api/message');

        setMessage(response.data.message);

      } catch (error) {

        console.error('Error fetching
message:', error);

      }

    };
```

```
    fetchMessage();

}, []);


return (
```

MERN App

```
{message}



  );

}



export default App;
```

This code fetches the message from the back-end API endpoint
and displays it in the front-end.

Deployment to Heroku

Now that we have our basic MERN application set up, let's deploy
it to Heroku.

1. Initialize a Git Repository

Initialize a Git repository in the root directory of your project:

```
git init
```

2. Create a Procfile

Heroku uses a file named `Procfile` (without any extension) to determine how to start your application. Create a file named `Procfile` in the root directory of your project and add the following line:

```
web: cd server && npm start
```

This line tells Heroku to navigate to the `server` directory and start the Node.js server using `npm start`.

3. Define Start Scripts

Modify the `package.json` files in both the `client` and `server` directories to include start scripts:

client/package.json:

```
{
```

```
  // ... other properties


  "scripts": {

    // ... other scripts


    "start": "react-scripts start",

    "build": "react-scripts build"
  },


  // ... other properties
}
```

server/package.json:

```
{

  // ... other properties


  "scripts": {

    // ... other scripts
```

```
    "start": "node index.js"
  },


  // ... other properties
}
```

These scripts define the commands to start the React development server and the Node.js server, respectively.

4. Create a Heroku App

Create a Heroku app using the Heroku CLI:

```
heroku create
```

This command will create a new Heroku app and associate it with your Git repository.

5. Set Environment Variables

Heroku allows you to set environment variables for your application. We'll set a variable named API_URL that our React front-end will use to communicate with our back-end API.

Set the API_URL environment variable using the Heroku CLI, replacing `your-heroku-app-name` with the name of your Heroku app:

```
heroku config:set API_URL=https://your-heroku-app-name.herokuapp.com
```

6. Modify React Front-End

Modify the App.js file in the client directory to use the API_URL environment variable:

```
import React, { useState, useEffect } from 'react';

import axios from 'axios';


function App() {

  const [message, setMessage] =
useState('');


  useEffect(() => {

    const fetchMessage = async () => {

      try {
```

```
        const response = await
axios.get(`${process.env.REACT_APP_API_URL}/
api/message`); // Use API_URL

        setMessage(response.data.message);

    } catch (error) {

        console.error('Error fetching
message:', error);

    }

    };


    fetchMessage();

  }, []);


  return (
```

MERN App

```
{message}



    );

}



export default App;
```

We use `process.env.REACT_APP_API_URL` to access the `API_URL` environment variable in our React front-end.

7. Build the React Front-End

Build the React front-end for production:

```
cd client

npm run build
```

This command will create a `build` directory within the `client` directory containing the production-ready build of our React front-end.

8. Deploy to Heroku

Commit your changes to Git and deploy to Heroku:

```
git add .

git commit -m "Initial deployment"

git push heroku master
```

This command will push your code to Heroku, which will then build and deploy your application.

9. Open the Application

Once the deployment is complete, you can open your application in your web browser by running:

```
heroku open
```

You should see your MERN application running on Heroku!

Troubleshooting Deployment Issues

Deployment can sometimes encounter issues. Here are some common troubleshooting tips:

- **Check Logs:** Heroku provides logs that can help you diagnose deployment issues. You can view the logs using the Heroku CLI: `heroku logs`.

- **Verify Environment Variables:** Ensure that you have set the necessary environment variables correctly.

- **Check Dependencies:** Make sure that all your application's dependencies are installed and specified correctly in your `package.json` files.

- **Read Documentation:** Consult the Heroku documentation for specific instructions and troubleshooting guides.

Continuous Integration and Continuous Deployment (CI/CD)

Continuous Integration and Continuous Deployment (CI/CD) are practices that automate the building, testing, and deployment of your application. CI/CD pipelines can help you streamline your development workflow, reduce errors, and ensure that your application is always up-to-date.

Heroku and other cloud platforms offer CI/CD tools and integrations that can automate your deployment process.

Deployment is a crucial step in the application development lifecycle, making your creations accessible to the world. Whether you choose shared hosting, VPS hosting, dedicated servers, or cloud platforms, understanding the different deployment options and their considerations is essential. Heroku provides a user-friendly platform for deploying MERN stack applications, offering a free tier that's suitable for small projects or prototypes. As you continue your journey in web development, embrace the power of deployment to bring your MERN stack applications to life and share them with the world.

Chapter Eighteen: Introduction to Redux for State Management

In the exciting world of building dynamic and interactive web applications with React, we often find ourselves juggling data that flows through various components. As our applications grow in complexity, managing this data efficiently becomes a paramount concern. Imagine building a large e-commerce application with numerous features like product listings, shopping carts, user profiles, and order management. Each of these features involves data that needs to be shared and synchronized across different parts of the application. Without a proper state management solution, we risk ending up with a tangled web of props drilling, component re-renders, and data inconsistencies.

Fortunately, the React ecosystem offers a powerful solution to this challenge: Redux. Redux is a predictable state management library for JavaScript applications, and it shines particularly brightly when used in conjunction with React. Redux provides a centralized store where we can keep all our application's state, making it easily accessible and manageable from any component. It enforces a unidirectional data flow, ensuring that changes to the state are predictable and traceable, making our applications easier to debug and maintain.

The Redux Philosophy: A Single Source of Truth

Redux embraces the concept of a single source of truth for your application's state. Imagine a library with a vast collection of books. Instead of having multiple copies of the same book scattered throughout the library, there's only one master copy of each book. If someone wants to borrow or return a book, they interact with this central collection, ensuring consistency and avoiding confusion.

In Redux, this central collection is called the store. The store holds the entire state of your application as a single JavaScript object.

Any component that needs access to the state can retrieve it from the store, and any component that needs to update the state must dispatch an action to the store.

Actions: Describing State Changes

Imagine you're sending a message to a friend. You write your message, put it in an envelope, address it, and send it off. The envelope represents the action in Redux. It's a plain JavaScript object that describes what happened in your application.

Actions have a `type` property that describes the type of action being performed. For example, if you're building a shopping cart application, you might have actions like `ADD_TO_CART`, `REMOVE_FROM_CART`, and `CHECKOUT`. The `type` property acts as a label that identifies the action.

Besides the `type` property, actions can carry additional data, often referred to as the payload. The payload contains the information necessary to perform the action. For instance, in the `ADD_TO_CART` action, the payload might include the product ID and quantity being added to the cart.

Reducers: Pure Functions for State Transformations

Once an action is dispatched, it's time for the reducer to step in. Reducers are pure functions that take the current state and an action as input and return a new state as output. They act as the state's transformation logic, determining how the state should change based on the action received.

Reducers are pure functions, meaning they don't have side effects and always return the same output for the same input. They don't modify the existing state directly but instead create a new state object based on the current state and the action.

Imagine a chef preparing a dish. The chef takes the ingredients (current state) and follows a recipe (action) to create a new dish (new state). The recipe doesn't change the original ingredients but instead guides the chef in creating something new.

The Store: Holding the State and Managing Actions

The store is the heart of Redux. It's responsible for holding the state, managing actions, and notifying subscribers about state changes. You create a store using the `createStore` function from Redux, passing it a reducer as an argument.

The store provides a few key methods for interacting with the state:

- `getState()`: Returns the current state of the store.

- `dispatch(action)`: Dispatches an action to the store. This triggers the reducer to update the state based on the action.

- `subscribe(listener)`: Subscribes a listener function to be notified whenever the state changes.

The Redux Flow: A Unidirectional Cycle

The Redux flow follows a unidirectional cycle:

- **Action:** An action is dispatched to describe a state change.

- **Reducer:** The reducer takes the current state and the action and returns a new state.

- **Store:** The store updates its state based on the new state returned by the reducer.

- **Subscribers:** The store notifies all subscribed listeners about the state change.

- **Components:** Components that are subscribed to the store's changes re-render to reflect the updated state.

262

This unidirectional data flow ensures that state changes are predictable and traceable, making our applications easier to debug and maintain.

Implementing Redux in a MERN Application

Let's illustrate how to implement Redux in a MERN stack application. We'll create a simple counter application where the user can increment and decrement a counter value.

1. Install Redux and React-Redux

First, we need to install the necessary Redux libraries. Open your terminal or command prompt, navigate to the root directory of your React front-end project (`client` in our previous deployment example), and run the following command:

```
npm install redux react-redux
```

This command will install the `redux` and `react-redux` libraries. `redux` provides the core Redux functionalities, while `react-redux` provides the bindings for integrating Redux with React.

2. Create a Redux Store

Create a new file named `store.js` in your `src` directory and add the following code:

```
import { createStore } from 'redux';
```

263

```javascript
// Define the initial state

const initialState = {

  count: 0,

};


// Define the reducer function

const counterReducer = (state =
initialState, action) => {

  switch (action.type) {

    case 'INCREMENT':

      return { ...state, count: state.count
+ 1 };

    case 'DECREMENT':

      return { ...state, count: state.count
- 1 };

    default:

      return state;

  }

};
```

```
// Create the Redux store

const store = createStore(counterReducer);


export default store;
```

In this code:

- We import the `createStore` function from `redux`.

- We define the initial state of our application as an object with a `count` property set to 0.

- We define the reducer function `counterReducer`, which takes the current state and an action as input and returns a new state based on the action's type.

- If the action type is `INCREMENT`, we increment the `count` by 1.

- If the action type is `DECREMENT`, we decrement the `count` by 1.

- If the action type is not recognized, we return the current state unchanged.

- We create the Redux store using `createStore(counterReducer)`.

3. Connect the Redux Store to React

Open your `index.js` file and modify it to connect the Redux store to our React application:

```jsx
import React from 'react';

import ReactDOM from 'react-dom/client';

import { Provider } from 'react-redux';

import App from './App';

import store from './store'; // Import the
Redux store

import './index.css';


const root =
ReactDOM.createRoot(document.getElementById(
'root'));

root.render(

  <React.StrictMode>

    <Provider store={store}> {/* Wrap the
App component with Provider */}

      <App />

    </Provider>

  </React.StrictMode>

);
```

In this code:

- We import the `Provider` component from `react-redux`.

- We wrap the `App` component with the `Provider` component, passing the `store` as a prop to the `Provider`. This makes the Redux store available to all components within the `App` component tree.

4. Create Action Creators

Action creators are functions that create actions. They provide a convenient way to dispatch actions from our components.

Create a new file named `actions.js` in your `src` directory and add the following code:

```
export const increment = () => ({

  type: 'INCREMENT',

});


export const decrement = () => ({

  type: 'DECREMENT',

});
```

In this code:

- We define two action creators, `increment` and `decrement`, that create actions of type `INCREMENT` and `DECREMENT`, respectively.

5. Connect Components to Redux

Now, let's modify our `App` component to connect it to Redux and use the action creators to dispatch actions. Open your `App.js` file and modify it as follows:

```
import React from 'react';

import { useSelector, useDispatch } from
'react-redux';

import { increment, decrement } from
'./actions';



function App() {

  const count = useSelector((state) =>
state.count); // Access the count from Redux
state

  const dispatch = useDispatch(); // Get the
dispatch function


  return (
```

Counter

```
Count: {count}

        dispatch(increment())}>Increment

        dispatch(decrement())}>Decrement




    );

}



export default App;
```

In this code:

- We import the useSelector and useDispatch
  Hooks from react-redux.

- `useSelector` allows us to access data from the Redux store. We use it to access the `count` value from the state.

- `useDispatch` gives us access to the `dispatch` function, which we can use to dispatch actions.

- We attach event handlers to the buttons that dispatch the `increment` and `decrement` actions using the action creators.

Save all the files and start your development server. You should now see a counter application where you can increment and decrement the counter value.

Conclusion

Redux provides a powerful and elegant solution for managing state in React applications. Its centralized store, unidirectional data flow, and use of pure functions make it a predictable and maintainable state management solution. By embracing Redux's concepts of actions, reducers, and the store, we can build complex and interactive React applications with ease, ensuring that data flows seamlessly through our components and state changes are traceable and predictable. As you continue your journey in React development, explore the rich ecosystem of Redux middleware, tools, and libraries to further enhance your state management capabilities and build applications that are both scalable and maintainable.

Chapter Nineteen: Connecting Redux to Your React Application

In the last chapter, we stepped into the world of Redux, a powerful state management library that brings order and predictability to the data flow in our React applications. We explored the core concepts of Redux: the store as the single source of truth, actions as messengers of state changes, and reducers as the architects of state transformations. We even created a simple counter application using Redux, demonstrating the fundamental principles of this elegant state management solution.

Now, it's time to delve deeper into the practical aspects of integrating Redux with our React applications. We'll learn how to connect our React components to the Redux store, allowing them to access the state, dispatch actions, and respond to state changes. We'll explore the `react-redux` library, a bridge that seamlessly connects the worlds of React and Redux, making the integration process smooth and intuitive.

React-Redux: The Bridge Between React and Redux

React-Redux is a library that provides the necessary bindings for integrating Redux with React. It acts as a translator, allowing our React components to communicate with the Redux store without having to deal with the low-level details of Redux. React-Redux provides two key components that are essential for this integration: the `<Provider>` component and the `connect` function.

The `<Provider>` Component: Making the Store Available

The `<Provider>` component from React-Redux acts as a global context provider for the Redux store. It makes the store accessible to all components within its subtree, ensuring that any component that needs access to the state or wants to dispatch actions can do so easily.

Think of the `<Provider>` component as a delivery service that brings the Redux store to the doorstep of every component within its reach. Any component that needs something from the store simply needs to place an order (using the `useSelector` Hook or the `connect` function), and the delivery service will bring it to them.

The `connect` Function: Connecting Components to the Store

The `connect` function from React-Redux is used to connect individual components to the Redux store. It takes two main arguments: `mapStateToProps` and `mapDispatchToProps`.

- **mapStateToProps:** This function defines how to extract the relevant data from the Redux store's state and make it available to the component as props. It takes the store's state as an argument and returns an object where the keys are the prop names and the values are the corresponding values from the state.

- **mapDispatchToProps:** This function defines how to dispatch actions to the Redux store from the component. It can take the `dispatch` function as an argument and return an object where the keys are the prop names (typically function names) and the values are the corresponding action creators or functions that dispatch actions.

Connecting a Component Using `connect`

Let's illustrate how to connect a component to the Redux store using the `connect` function. Suppose we have a `Counter` component that displays the current count value and two buttons for incrementing and decrementing the count.

```
import React from 'react';
```

```javascript
import { connect } from 'react-redux';

import { increment, decrement } from
'./actions';


function Counter(props) {

  return (

    <div>

      <h1>Counter</h1>

      <p>Count: {props.count}</p>

      <button
onClick={props.increment}>Increment</button>

      <button
onClick={props.decrement}>Decrement</button>

    </div>

  );

}


// Map Redux state to component props

const mapStateToProps = (state) => ({

  count: state.count,

});
```

```
// Map Redux dispatch to component props

const mapDispatchToProps = {

  increment: increment,

  decrement: decrement,

};


// Connect the component to the Redux store

export default connect(mapStateToProps,
mapDispatchToProps)(Counter);
```

In this code:

- We import the `connect` function from `react-redux`.

- We define the `Counter` component, which receives the `count`, `increment`, and `decrement` props from the Redux store.

- We define the `mapStateToProps` function, which extracts the `count` value from the Redux state and makes it available to the component as the `count` prop.

- We define the `mapDispatchToProps` object, which maps the `increment` and `decrement` action creators to the `increment` and `decrement` props, respectively.

- We call `connect(mapStateToProps, mapDispatchToProps)(Counter)` to connect the `Counter` component to the Redux store. The `connect` function returns a new, enhanced component that is connected to the store.

Now, when the `Counter` component is rendered, it will have access to the `count`, `increment`, and `decrement` props from the Redux store. The `count` prop will display the current count value, and clicking the buttons will dispatch the `increment` and `decrement` actions, updating the Redux state and causing the component to re-render with the updated count value.

Accessing the Store with `useSelector`

React-Redux provides another way to access data from the Redux store within functional components: the `useSelector` Hook. The `useSelector` Hook allows you to extract data from the store's state and subscribe to its changes.

Let's refactor our `Counter` component to use the `useSelector` Hook:

```
import React from 'react';

import { useSelector, useDispatch } from
'react-redux';

import { increment, decrement } from
'./actions';


function Counter() {
```

```
  const count = useSelector((state) =>
state.count);

  const dispatch = useDispatch();


  return (

    <div>

      <h1>Counter</h1>

      <p>Count: {count}</p>

      <button onClick={() =>
dispatch(increment())}>Increment</button>

        <button onClick={() =>
dispatch(decrement())}>Decrement</button>

      </div>

  );

}


export default Counter;
```

In this code:

- We import the useSelector and useDispatch
  Hooks from react-redux.

- We use the `useSelector` Hook to access the `count` value from the Redux state. The `useSelector` Hook takes a selector function as an argument, which receives the Redux state and returns the desired data.

- We use the `useDispatch` Hook to get access to the `dispatch` function, which we can use to dispatch actions to the Redux store.

Choosing Between `connect` and `useSelector`

Both the `connect` function and the `useSelector` Hook provide ways to access data from the Redux store. The choice between them depends on your preference and the specific scenario.

- **connect:** The `connect` function is a powerful tool for connecting class components to the Redux store. It allows you to map both state and dispatch to component props, making it suitable for components that need both access to the state and the ability to dispatch actions.

- **useSelector:** The `useSelector` Hook is a more concise and modern approach for accessing the Redux store within functional components. It's suitable for components that only need to read data from the store and don't need to dispatch actions directly.

Handling Complex State Structures

In real-world applications, the Redux state is often more complex than a single value. It might be an object with nested properties or an array of objects. Both `mapStateToProps` and `useSelector` can handle these complex state structures.

Let's illustrate this with an example. Suppose we have a Redux state that stores a list of to-do items:

```
const initialState = {

  todos: [

    { id: 1, text: 'Learn Redux', completed:
false },

    { id: 2, text: 'Build a to-do app',
completed: true },

  ],

};
```

We can access the to-do items in our TodoList component using mapStateToProps:

```
import React from 'react';

import { connect } from 'react-redux';


function TodoList(props) {
  return (
    <ul>
      {props.todos.map((todo) => (
        <li key={todo.id}>{todo.text}</li>
```

```
    ) ) }

  </ul>

 ) ;

}


const mapStateToProps = (state) => ({

  todos: state.todos,

});


export default
connect(mapStateToProps)(TodoList);
```

Alternatively, we can use `useSelector`:

```
import React from 'react';

import { useSelector } from 'react-redux';


function TodoList() {

  const todos = useSelector((state) =>
state.todos);
```

```
    return (

      <ul>

        {todos.map((todo) => (

          <li key={todo.id}>{todo.text}</li>

        ))}

      </ul>

    );

}


export default TodoList;
```

Dispatching Actions with `mapDispatchToProps`

The `mapDispatchToProps` argument to the `connect` function allows us to map action creators or functions that dispatch actions to component props. This makes it easy to dispatch actions from our components without having to directly access the `dispatch` function.

Let's revisit our `Counter` component and map the `increment` and `decrement` action creators to component props:

```
import React from 'react';

import { connect } from 'react-redux';

import { increment, decrement } from
'./actions';


function Counter(props) {

  return (

    <div>

      <h1>Counter</h1>

      <p>Count: {props.count}</p>

      <button
onClick={props.increment}>Increment</button>

      <button
onClick={props.decrement}>Decrement</button>

    </div>

  );

}


const mapStateToProps = (state) => ({

  count: state.count,

});
```

```
const mapDispatchToProps = {

  increment: increment,

  decrement: decrement,

};



export default connect(mapStateToProps,
mapDispatchToProps)(Counter);
```

In this code:

- The `mapDispatchToProps` object maps the
  `increment` and `decrement` action creators to the
  `increment` and `decrement` props, respectively.

- Now, when we call `props.increment()` or
  `props.decrement()` in the component, it will dispatch
  the corresponding action to the Redux store.

Dispatching Actions with `useDispatch`

As we saw earlier, the `useDispatch` Hook provides a
convenient way to dispatch actions from functional components.
We can use it in conjunction with action creators to dispatch
actions to the Redux store.

Let's refactor our `Counter` component to use `useDispatch`:

```
import React from 'react';

import { useSelector, useDispatch } from
'react-redux';

import { increment, decrement } from
'./actions';


function Counter() {

  const count = useSelector((state) =>
state.count);

  const dispatch = useDispatch();


  return (

    <div>

      <h1>Counter</h1>

      <p>Count: {count}</p>

      <button onClick={() =>
dispatch(increment())}>Increment</button>

      <button onClick={() =>
dispatch(decrement())}>Decrement</button>

    </div>

  );

}
```

```
export default Counter;
```

In this code:

- We use the `useDispatch` Hook to get access to the `dispatch` function.

- We call `dispatch(increment())` or `dispatch(decrement())` to dispatch the corresponding actions.

Passing Props to Action Creators

Sometimes, we need to pass additional data to action creators. For example, if we're building a to-do application, we might want to pass the text of the new to-do item to the action creator that adds a new to-do.

We can achieve this by creating action creators that accept arguments. Let's modify our `addTodo` action creator to accept the to-do text as an argument:

```
export const addTodo = (text) => ({

  type: 'ADD_TODO',

  payload: { text },

});
```

Now, we can pass the to-do text to the action creator when we dispatch the action:

```
dispatch(addTodo('Learn Redux'));
```

Conclusion

Integrating Redux with React using the `react-redux` library provides a powerful and elegant way to manage state in our React applications. The `<Provider>` component makes the Redux store globally accessible, and the `connect` function and the `useSelector` and `useDispatch` Hooks allow our components to interact with the store, accessing state, dispatching actions, and responding to state changes. By mastering these techniques, we can build complex and interactive React applications with ease, ensuring that our data flow is predictable, traceable, and manageable. As you delve deeper into the world of Redux, explore its advanced features, middleware, and best practices to further enhance your state management skills and build applications that are both scalable and maintainable.

Chapter Twenty: Working with Asynchronous Actions in Redux

In our exploration of Redux, we've gained valuable insights into how it brings order and predictability to state management in React applications. We've learned to create a centralized store, dispatch actions to describe state changes, and use reducers to transform the state based on these actions. We've even seen how to connect our React components to the Redux store, allowing them to access the state, dispatch actions, and respond to state changes. However, our examples so far have primarily dealt with synchronous actions, those that update the state immediately. In the real world, many operations involve asynchronous tasks, such as fetching data from an API, performing time-consuming calculations, or interacting with external services. These asynchronous actions require a slightly different approach to ensure that our Redux state remains consistent and our application behaves as expected.

Embracing Asynchronous Operations: The Real World of Web Apps

Asynchronous operations are the backbone of modern web applications. They allow us to perform tasks that take time to complete without blocking the user interface, ensuring a smooth and responsive user experience. Imagine fetching a list of products from an API, uploading a large file, or sending an email. These operations don't happen instantaneously; they require time to process, and we don't want our users to stare at a frozen screen while they wait.

JavaScript provides various mechanisms for handling asynchronous operations, such as callbacks, promises, and async/await. However, integrating these mechanisms with Redux requires careful consideration to maintain the predictable state updates that Redux is known for.

Challenges of Asynchronous Actions in Redux

When dealing with asynchronous actions in Redux, we face a few challenges:

- **State Updates:** Asynchronous actions don't update the state immediately. They might take some time to complete, and we need to handle the intermediate states while the operation is in progress.

- **Error Handling:** Asynchronous operations can fail, and we need to handle these errors gracefully, updating the state to reflect the error condition.

- **Data Consistency:** Asynchronous actions might update the state multiple times, and we need to ensure that these updates happen in the correct order and don't conflict with each other.

Redux Thunk: Middleware for Asynchronous Actions

Redux Thunk is a middleware library that enables us to handle asynchronous actions in Redux. Middleware, in the context of Redux, are functions that intercept actions before they reach the reducer. They allow us to extend Redux's functionality by adding custom logic to the action dispatching process.

Redux Thunk specifically allows action creators to return functions instead of plain action objects. These functions can then perform asynchronous tasks, such as fetching data from an API, and dispatch actions when the task is complete.

Installing Redux Thunk

Before we can use Redux Thunk, we need to install it. Open your terminal or command prompt, navigate to the root directory of your React front-end project (`client` in our previous deployment example), and run the following command:

```
npm install redux-thunk
```

Applying Redux Thunk Middleware

Once Redux Thunk is installed, we need to apply it as middleware to our Redux store. Open your `store.js` file and modify it as follows:

```
import { createStore, applyMiddleware } from
'redux';

import thunk from 'redux-thunk';

import counterReducer from './reducer'; //
Assuming your reducer is in reducer.js


const store = createStore(counterReducer,
applyMiddleware(thunk));


export default store;
```

In this code:

- We import the `applyMiddleware` function from redux.

- We import the `thunk` middleware from `redux-thunk`.

- We create the Redux store using `createStore(counterReducer, applyMiddleware(thunk))`. The `applyMiddleware` function applies the `thunk` middleware to the store.

Creating an Asynchronous Action Creator

Now, let's create an asynchronous action creator that fetches data from an API. Suppose we have an API endpoint that returns a random quote. We can create an action creator to fetch this quote and update the Redux state with the fetched data.

Create a new file named `actions.js` in your `src` directory and add the following code:

```
export const fetchQuote = () => {

  return async (dispatch) => {

    dispatch({ type: 'FETCH_QUOTE_REQUEST'
}); // Dispatch a request action


    try {

      const response = await
fetch('https://api.quotable.io/random');

      const data = await response.json();
```

```
      dispatch({ type:
'FETCH_QUOTE_SUCCESS', payload: data.content
}); // Dispatch a success action with the
fetched quote

    } catch (error) {

      dispatch({ type:
'FETCH_QUOTE_FAILURE', payload:
error.message }); // Dispatch a failure
action with the error message

    }

  };

};
```

In this code:

- We define an action creator `fetchQuote` that returns a function.

- The returned function takes the `dispatch` function as an argument. This allows the function to dispatch actions to the Redux store.

- We dispatch a FETCH_QUOTE_REQUEST action to indicate that the quote fetching process has started.

- We use `fetch` to make a GET request to the API endpoint.

- We wrap the `fetch` call in a `try...catch` block to handle potential errors.

- If the request is successful, we dispatch a
  FETCH_QUOTE_SUCCESS action with the fetched quote
  as the payload.

- If an error occurs, we dispatch a
  FETCH_QUOTE_FAILURE action with the error message
  as the payload.

Handling Asynchronous Actions in the Reducer

Now, let's modify our reducer to handle the asynchronous actions
we've defined. Assuming your reducer is in reducer.js,
modify it as follows:

```
const initialState = {

  quote: '',

  loading: false,

  error: null,

};
```

```
const quoteReducer = (state = initialState,
action) => {

  switch (action.type) {

    case 'FETCH_QUOTE_REQUEST':

      return { ...state, loading: true,
error: null };

    case 'FETCH_QUOTE_SUCCESS':
```

```
      return { ...state, quote:
action.payload, loading: false, error: null
};

    case 'FETCH_QUOTE_FAILURE':

      return { ...state, quote: '', loading:
false, error: action.payload };

    default:

      return state;

  }

};



export default quoteReducer;
```

In this code:

- We add `loading` and `error` properties to the initial state to track the loading status and any errors during the quote fetching process.

- We handle the FETCH_QUOTE_REQUEST, FETCH_QUOTE_SUCCESS, and FETCH_QUOTE_FAILURE actions, updating the state accordingly.

Using the Asynchronous Action Creator

Now, let's use our asynchronous action creator in a component. Suppose we have a `Quote` component that displays the fetched quote, a loading indicator while the quote is being fetched, and an error message if an error occurs.

```
import React, { useEffect } from 'react';

import { useSelector, useDispatch } from
'react-redux';

import { fetchQuote } from './actions';


function Quote() {

  const quote = useSelector((state) =>
state.quote);

  const loading = useSelector((state) =>
state.loading);

  const error = useSelector((state) =>
state.error);

  const dispatch = useDispatch();


  useEffect(() => {

    dispatch(fetchQuote()); // Dispatch the
fetchQuote action when the component mounts

  }, [dispatch]);
```

```
if (loading) {

  return <p>Loading quote...</p>;

}


if (error) {

  return <p>Error: {error}</p>;

}


return (

  <div>

    <h1>Random Quote</h1>

    <p>{quote}</p>

  </div>

);

}


export default Quote;
```

In this code:

- We use the `useSelector` Hook to access the `quote`, `loading`, and `error` values from the Redux state.

- We use the `useDispatch` Hook to get access to the `dispatch` function.

- We use the `useEffect` Hook to dispatch the `fetchQuote` action when the component mounts.

- We conditionally render different content based on the `loading` and `error` states.

Save all the files and start your development server. You should now see a random quote being fetched from the API and displayed in the component.

Redux Promise Middleware: Handling Promises Directly

Redux Promise Middleware is another middleware library that simplifies handling asynchronous actions that return promises. It allows you to dispatch promises directly as actions, and the middleware will handle resolving or rejecting the promise and dispatching the appropriate actions.

Installing Redux Promise Middleware

To use Redux Promise Middleware, install it using the following command:

```
npm install redux-promise-middleware
```

Applying Redux Promise Middleware

Once installed, apply the middleware to your Redux store:

```
import { createStore, applyMiddleware } from
'redux';

import promiseMiddleware from 'redux-
promise-middleware';

import quoteReducer from './reducer';


const store = createStore(quoteReducer,
applyMiddleware(promiseMiddleware));


export default store;
```

Creating a Promise-Based Action Creator

Now, let's create a promise-based action creator:

```
export const fetchQuote = () => {

  return {

    type: 'FETCH_QUOTE',

    payload:
fetch('https://api.quotable.io/random').then
((response) =>
```

```
        response.json()

    ),

  };

};
```

In this code:

- We define an action creator `fetchQuote` that returns an object with the action type `FETCH_QUOTE` and a payload that's a promise.

- The promise fetches the quote from the API and resolves with the JSON data.

Handling Promise-Based Actions in the Reducer

Redux Promise Middleware automatically dispatches three actions for each promise-based action:

- `FETCH_QUOTE_PENDING`: Dispatched when the promise is pending.

- `FETCH_QUOTE_FULFILLED`: Dispatched when the promise is fulfilled.

- `FETCH_QUOTE_REJECTED`: Dispatched when the promise is rejected.

We need to handle these actions in our reducer:

```
const initialState = {

  quote: '',

  loading: false,

  error: null,

};


const quoteReducer = (state = initialState,
action) => {

  switch (action.type) {

    case 'FETCH_QUOTE_PENDING':

      return { ...state, loading: true,
error: null };

    case 'FETCH_QUOTE_FULFILLED':

      return { ...state, quote:
action.payload.content, loading: false,
error: null };

    case 'FETCH_QUOTE_REJECTED':

      return { ...state, quote: '', loading:
false, error: action.payload };

    default:

      return state;

  }
```

```
};
```

```
export default quoteReducer;
```

Redux Saga: Managing Side Effects with Sagas

Redux Saga is another powerful middleware library that provides a way to manage side effects in Redux applications using sagas. Sagas are generator functions that listen for specific actions and perform side effects, such as fetching data from an API, in response to those actions.

Installing Redux Saga

To use Redux Saga, install it using the following command:

```
npm install redux-saga
```

Applying Redux Saga Middleware

Once installed, apply the middleware to your Redux store:

```
import { createStore, applyMiddleware } from
'redux';
```

```
import createSagaMiddleware from 'redux-
saga';

import quoteReducer from './reducer';

import rootSaga from './sagas'; // Assuming
your sagas are in sagas.js


const sagaMiddleware =
createSagaMiddleware();

const store = createStore(quoteReducer,
applyMiddleware(sagaMiddleware));


sagaMiddleware.run(rootSaga); // Run the
root saga


export default store;
```

Creating a Saga

Let's create a saga to fetch the random quote:

```
import { call, put, takeEvery } from 'redux-
saga/effects';
```

```javascript
function* fetchQuoteSaga() {

  try {

    const response = yield call(fetch,
'https://api.quotable.io/random');

    const data = yield call([response,
'json']);



    yield put({ type: 'FETCH_QUOTE_SUCCESS',
payload: data.content });

  } catch (error) {

    yield put({ type: 'FETCH_QUOTE_FAILURE',
payload: error.message });

  }

}



function* rootSaga() {

  yield takeEvery('FETCH_QUOTE_REQUEST',
fetchQuoteSaga);

}



export default rootSaga;
```

In this code:

- We import the `call`, `put`, and `takeEvery` effects from `redux-saga/effects`.

- `call` is used to call a function, such as `fetch`.

- `put` is used to dispatch an action to the Redux store.

- `takeEvery` listens for a specific action type and executes a saga whenever that action is dispatched.

- We define a saga `fetchQuoteSaga` that fetches the quote from the API.

- We define a root saga `rootSaga` that listens for the `FETCH_QUOTE_REQUEST` action and executes the `fetchQuoteSaga` whenever it's dispatched.

Dispatching the Action

We can now dispatch the `FETCH_QUOTE_REQUEST` action from our component:

```
import React, { useEffect } from 'react';

import { useSelector, useDispatch } from
'react-redux';


function Quote() {

  // ... (other code)
```

```
useEffect(() => {

   dispatch({ type: 'FETCH_QUOTE_REQUEST'
}); // Dispatch the request action

}, [dispatch]);


// ... (other code)

}


export default Quote;
```

Choosing the Right Middleware for Asynchronous Actions

Redux Thunk, Redux Promise Middleware, and Redux Saga all offer different approaches to handling asynchronous actions in Redux. The best choice for your application depends on your specific needs and preferences.

- **Redux Thunk:** A simple and lightweight middleware that's suitable for basic asynchronous operations.

- **Redux Promise Middleware:** Simplifies handling promises directly as actions.

- **Redux Saga:** A more powerful middleware that provides a declarative way to manage side effects using sagas.

Asynchronous operations are an integral part of modern web applications, enabling us to perform time-consuming tasks without blocking the user interface. Integrating asynchronous actions with Redux requires careful consideration to maintain the predictable state updates that Redux is known for. Redux Thunk, Redux Promise Middleware, and Redux Saga offer powerful solutions for handling asynchronous actions, providing different approaches to managing side effects, state updates, and error handling. By understanding these middleware libraries and their strengths, we can choose the best approach for our specific needs and build robust and responsive React applications that seamlessly handle asynchronous operations.

Chapter Twenty-One: Testing Your MERN Stack Application

Throughout our journey of building MERN stack applications, we've witnessed the power of combining MongoDB, Express.js, React.js, and Node.js to create dynamic and interactive web experiences. We've learned to craft robust back-ends, dynamic front-ends, manage application state, fetch data from APIs, handle routing, and implement security measures. However, as our applications grow in complexity, ensuring their reliability and correctness becomes increasingly crucial. Just like a skilled craftsperson meticulously examines their work for flaws and imperfections, we need to rigorously test our applications to catch bugs, prevent regressions, and maintain a high level of quality. This chapter will guide you through the world of testing in MERN stack applications, exploring different types of tests, popular testing frameworks, and best practices for incorporating testing into your development workflow.

Testing: Ensuring Reliability and Correctness

Testing is the process of evaluating and verifying that your application behaves as expected. It involves writing code that executes different parts of your application and checks if the output matches the expected results. Testing is an integral part of the software development lifecycle, as it helps us catch bugs early in the development process, prevents regressions (reintroducing previously fixed bugs), and ensures that our applications meet the required quality standards.

Testing can be viewed as a safety net that catches potential issues before they reach our users. Just as a bridge undergoes rigorous stress testing to ensure its structural integrity, testing our applications helps us identify weaknesses and vulnerabilities, allowing us to address them before they cause problems.

Types of Tests: A Spectrum of Coverage

In the world of software testing, there are various types of tests, each focusing on different aspects of the application. The most common types of tests in MERN stack applications are:

- **Unit Tests:** Unit tests focus on testing individual units of code, such as functions or components, in isolation. They aim to verify that each unit of code works as expected, independent of other parts of the application. Unit tests are like testing the individual gears of a clock to ensure that each gear functions correctly on its own.

- **Integration Tests:** Integration tests focus on testing the interactions between different units of code, such as how multiple components work together or how the front-end interacts with the back-end API. They aim to verify that the different parts of the application integrate seamlessly and work together as expected. Integration tests are like testing the entire clock mechanism to ensure that all the gears mesh together and the clock keeps accurate time.

- **End-to-End (E2E) Tests:** End-to-End tests focus on testing the entire application flow from the user's perspective. They simulate real user interactions, such as navigating through the application, filling out forms, and interacting with different features, to verify that the application behaves as expected from start to finish. End-to-End tests are like testing the clock by observing its hands and listening to its ticking to ensure that it displays the correct time and sounds as expected.

Testing Frameworks: Tools of the Trade

The JavaScript ecosystem offers a wide range of testing frameworks and libraries that simplify the process of writing and running tests. Some popular testing frameworks for MERN stack applications include:

Jest: A Comprehensive Testing Framework

Jest is a comprehensive and widely used JavaScript testing framework developed by Facebook. It provides a rich set of features, including:

- **Test Runner:** Jest includes a test runner that executes your tests and reports the results.

- **Assertion Library:** Jest provides a built-in assertion library that allows you to make assertions about the expected behavior of your code.

- **Mocking:** Jest offers powerful mocking capabilities that allow you to isolate units of code by replacing dependencies with mock objects.

- **Code Coverage:** Jest can generate code coverage reports that show you how much of your code is covered by your tests.

- **Snapshot Testing:** Jest supports snapshot testing, which allows you to capture the rendered output of a component and compare it to a previous snapshot, ensuring that the component's output hasn't changed unexpectedly.

Mocha: A Flexible Testing Framework

Mocha is another popular JavaScript testing framework known for its flexibility and extensibility. It provides a core test runner and assertion library, allowing you to choose other libraries for mocking, code coverage, and other functionalities.

Chai: An Assertion Library

Chai is a popular assertion library that can be used with various testing frameworks, including Jest and Mocha. It provides a variety of assertion styles, allowing you to choose the style that best suits your preference and coding style.

Supertest: Testing HTTP APIs

Supertest is a library that simplifies testing HTTP APIs. It provides a fluent API for making HTTP requests to your API endpoints and making assertions about the responses.

Unit Testing React Components with Jest and React Testing Library

Let's start with an example of unit testing React components using Jest and React Testing Library. React Testing Library is a library that encourages testing React components from the user's perspective, focusing on how the component interacts with the user rather than its internal implementation.

Suppose we have a simple `Counter` component that displays a counter value and two buttons for incrementing and decrementing the count:

```
import React, { useState } from 'react';


function Counter() {

  const [count, setCount] = useState(0);


  const increment = () => {

    setCount(count + 1);
```

```
  };


  const decrement = () => {

    setCount(count - 1);

  };


  return (

    <div>

      <h1>Counter</h1>

      <p>Count: {count}</p>

      <button
onClick={increment}>Increment</button>

      <button
onClick={decrement}>Decrement</button>

    </div>

  );

}


export default Counter;
```

We can write a unit test for this component using Jest and React Testing Library as follows:

```
import React from 'react';

import { render, screen, fireEvent } from
'@testing-library/react';

import Counter from './Counter';


test('counter increments and decrements
correctly', () => {

  render(<Counter />); // Render the Counter
component


  // Get references to the elements we want
to interact with

  const countElement =
screen.getByText(/Count: 0/i); // Find the
element with the text "Count: 0"

  const incrementButton =
screen.getByRole('button', { name:
/Increment/i }); // Find the increment
button

  const decrementButton =
screen.getByRole('button', { name:
/Decrement/i }); // Find the decrement
button
```

```
// Assert that the initial count is 0

expect(countElement).toHaveTextContent('Coun
t: 0');


// Click the increment button

fireEvent.click(incrementButton);


// Assert that the count has incremented
to 1

expect(countElement).toHaveTextContent('Coun
t: 1');


// Click the decrement button

fireEvent.click(decrementButton);


// Assert that the count has decremented
back to 0

expect(countElement).toHaveTextContent('Coun
t: 0');

});
```

In this test:

- We use the `render` function from React Testing Library to render the `Counter` component.

- We use the `screen` object to query the rendered component for specific elements.

- `screen.getByText(/Count: 0/i)` finds the element with the text "Count: 0," ignoring case.

- `screen.getByRole('button', { name: /Increment/i })` finds the button with the role "button" and the name "Increment," ignoring case.

- `screen.getByRole('button', { name: /Decrement/i })` finds the button with the role "button" and the name "Decrement," ignoring case.

- We use the `fireEvent` object to simulate user interactions, such as clicking the buttons.

- We use Jest's `expect` function to make assertions about the expected behavior of the component.

- `expect(countElement).toHaveTextContent('Count: 0')` asserts that the `countElement` has the text content "Count: 0."

This test simulates user interactions with the `Counter` component, clicking the buttons and verifying that the count value updates correctly.

Testing Redux Actions and Reducers

We can also write unit tests for our Redux actions and reducers. Action tests typically verify that the action creator returns the expected action object, while reducer tests verify that the reducer updates the state correctly based on the action received.

Testing Actions

Let's write a unit test for our `increment` action creator:

```
import { increment } from './actions';



test('increment action creator returns the correct action', () => {

  const expectedAction = { type: 'INCREMENT' };


  expect(increment()).toEqual(expectedAction);

});
```

In this test:

- We import the `increment` action creator from our `actions` file.

- We define the expected action object.

- We use Jest's `expect` function to assert that the `increment()` function returns the expected action object.

Testing Reducers

Now, let's write a unit test for our counter reducer:

```
import counterReducer from './reducer';
```

```
test('counter reducer increments the count',
() => {

  const initialState = { count: 0 };

  const action = { type: 'INCREMENT' };

  const expectedState = { count: 1 };

  expect(counterReducer(initialState,
action)).toEqual(expectedState);

});
```

```
test('counter reducer decrements the count',
() => {

  const initialState = { count: 1 };

  const action = { type: 'DECREMENT' };

  const expectedState = { count: 0 };

  expect(counterReducer(initialState,
action)).toEqual(expectedState);

});
```

In these tests:

- We import the `counterReducer` from our `reducer` file.

- We define the initial state and the action object.

- We define the expected state after the reducer has processed the action.

- We use Jest's `expect` function to assert that the `counterReducer` function returns the expected state.

Integration Testing with Supertest

Integration tests verify that different parts of our application work together as expected. For example, we can write integration tests to verify that our front-end can communicate with our back-end API and that the data is processed correctly.

Let's write an integration test using Supertest to verify that our back-end API endpoint `/api/message` returns the expected response:

```
const request = require('supertest');

const app = require('./index'); // Assuming
your Express app is in index.js


describe('GET /api/message', () => {
```

```
it('should return a 200 status code and
the expected message', async () => {

    const response = await
request(app).get('/api/message');


    expect(response.status).toBe(200);

    expect(response.body).toEqual({ message:
'Hello from the server!' });

  });

});
```

In this test:

- We use the `request` function from Supertest to make a GET request to the `/api/message` endpoint.

- We use Jest's `expect` function to assert that:

- The response status code is 200 (OK).

- The response body is a JSON object with the expected message.

This test verifies that our back-end API endpoint is working correctly and returning the expected data.

End-to-End Testing with Cypress

End-to-End tests simulate real user interactions with our application, verifying that the entire application flow works as expected. Cypress is a popular end-to-end testing framework that provides a rich set of features for testing web applications.

Installing Cypress

To use Cypress, install it using the following command:

```
npm install cypress --save-dev
```

Running Cypress

Once Cypress is installed, you can open the Cypress Test Runner by running the following command:

```
npx cypress open
```

This will open the Cypress Test Runner, where you can create and run your end-to-end tests.

Writing an End-to-End Test

Let's write an end-to-end test that simulates a user visiting our counter application, incrementing the count, and verifying that the count value updates correctly in the UI.

Create a new file named counter.spec.js in the cypress/integration directory and add the following code:

317

```
describe('Counter App', () => {

  it('increments the count correctly', () =>
{

    cy.visit('http://localhost:3000'); //
Visit the application



    cy.get('h1').should('contain',
'Counter'); // Assert that the heading
contains "Counter"

    cy.get('p').should('contain', 'Count:
0'); // Assert that the initial count is 0



cy.get('button').contains('Increment').click
(); // Click the "Increment" button



    cy.get('p').should('contain', 'Count:
1'); // Assert that the count has
incremented to 1

  });

});
```

In this test:

- We use the `cy.visit()` command to visit the application running on `http://localhost:3000`.

- We use the `cy.get()` command to query the DOM for specific elements.

- `cy.get('h1')` finds the `<h1>` element.

- `cy.get('p')` finds the `<p>` element that displays the count.

- `cy.get('button').contains('Increment')` finds the button that contains the text "Increment."

- We use the `cy.should()` command to make assertions about the elements.

- `cy.get('h1').should('contain', 'Counter')` asserts that the `<h1>` element contains the text "Counter."

- `cy.get('p').should('contain', 'Count: 0')` asserts that the `<p>` element contains the text "Count: 0."

- We use the `cy.click()` command to simulate a user clicking the "Increment" button.

This test simulates a user interacting with our counter application and verifies that the count value updates correctly in the UI.

Testing Best Practices

Here are some best practices for incorporating testing into your MERN stack application development workflow:

- **Test Early and Often:** Start writing tests early in the development process and run them frequently to catch bugs early and prevent regressions.

- **Focus on User Interactions:** When testing React components, focus on how the component interacts with the user rather than its internal implementation.

- **Use Descriptive Test Names:** Choose descriptive names for your tests that clearly explain what the test is verifying.

- **Keep Tests Concise:** Keep your tests concise and focused on a single aspect of the application.

- **Mock Dependencies:** Use mocking to isolate units of code and avoid testing dependencies.

- **Measure Code Coverage:** Use code coverage reports to track how much of your code is covered by your tests and identify areas that need more testing.

- **Integrate with CI/CD:** Integrate testing into your continuous integration and continuous deployment (CI/CD) pipeline to ensure that tests are run automatically whenever code changes are pushed.

Testing is a cornerstone of building reliable and high-quality MERN stack applications. It helps us catch bugs early, prevent regressions, and ensure that our applications meet the required quality standards. By understanding different types of tests, popular testing frameworks, and best practices for incorporating testing into our development workflow, we can build robust and trustworthy applications that our users can rely on. As you continue your journey in web development, embrace testing as an essential part of your development process, ensuring that your applications are thoroughly vetted and ready to face the challenges of the real world.

Chapter Twenty-Two: Improving Performance and Scalability

In our journey through the MERN stack, we've covered a wide spectrum of topics, from the foundational concepts of each technology to building complete applications, handling data, routing, authentication, and even testing. Our applications are functional and ready to serve users, but as they grow in complexity and user base, performance and scalability become paramount considerations. Just as a well-designed bridge can handle increasing traffic without collapsing, our applications need to be architected and optimized to handle a growing number of users and requests without compromising speed or reliability. This chapter will delve into strategies and techniques for enhancing the performance and scalability of your MERN stack applications, ensuring they remain responsive and robust even as they scale to accommodate a larger audience and handle heavier workloads.

Performance Optimization: The Need for Speed

Performance is a critical aspect of user experience. Users expect web applications to be fast and responsive, loading quickly and handling interactions smoothly. Slow loading times, sluggish interactions, and frequent delays can lead to frustration, abandonment, and ultimately, a negative impact on your application's success.

Think of performance optimization as fine-tuning a race car. Every component, from the engine to the tires, needs to be meticulously optimized to minimize friction, maximize efficiency, and achieve peak performance. Similarly, in MERN stack applications, we need to optimize every layer, from the database to the front-end, to deliver a snappy and delightful user experience.

Optimizing the Back-end: Express.js and MongoDB

The back-end is often the bottleneck for performance in web applications. It handles data processing, database interactions, and business logic, and any inefficiencies in these areas can significantly impact the overall performance of the application. Let's explore some strategies for optimizing our Express.js back-end and MongoDB database.

Caching: Reducing Redundant Operations

Caching is a technique that involves storing frequently accessed data in a temporary storage area, such as memory or a dedicated caching server, to reduce the need for redundant operations. When a request arrives for data that's already cached, the server can retrieve it from the cache instead of performing the potentially time-consuming operation of fetching it from the database or performing complex calculations.

Imagine a library with a limited number of copies of a popular book. Every time someone wants to borrow the book, they have to wait in line. To improve efficiency, the library could create a separate shelf near the entrance with multiple copies of the popular book. Now, people who want to borrow the book can quickly grab a copy from the shelf without waiting in the main line.

In Express.js, we can implement caching using middleware, such as `express-redis-cache` or `memory-cache`. These middleware libraries allow us to cache API responses, reducing the load on our database and speeding up response times.

Database Indexing: Speeding Up Queries

Database queries are often a major source of performance bottlenecks. When querying large datasets, unindexed queries can take a significant amount of time to complete, slowing down our application. Database indexing is a technique that creates data structures that allow the database to quickly locate the required data, speeding up query performance.

Think of a dictionary. If you want to find a specific word, you don't have to read the entire dictionary from beginning to end. Instead, you use the index, which provides a quick way to locate the word based on its first letter.

In MongoDB, we can create indexes on fields that are frequently used in queries. Indexes allow MongoDB to quickly locate the relevant documents, reducing query times and improving performance.

Query Optimization: Writing Efficient Queries

Even with indexed fields, the efficiency of our database queries plays a crucial role in performance. Writing efficient queries that retrieve only the necessary data and avoid unnecessary operations can significantly impact query times.

Some tips for writing efficient MongoDB queries include:

- **Use Projection:** Specify the fields you need in the query's projection to retrieve only the required data, reducing the amount of data transferred from the database.

- **Use Limits:** Use the `limit` operator to limit the number of documents returned, especially when dealing with large datasets.

- **Avoid $where:** The `$where` operator allows you to use JavaScript code in your queries, but it can significantly slow down query performance. Use other query operators whenever possible.

Asynchronous Operations: Keeping the Back-end Responsive

Asynchronous operations, such as fetching data from external APIs or performing time-consuming calculations, can block the execution of other tasks, slowing down our back-end. JavaScript's asynchronous nature allows us to perform these operations without blocking, ensuring that our back-end remains responsive and can handle multiple requests concurrently.

In Express.js, we can use promises or async/await to handle asynchronous operations. These mechanisms allow us to initiate an asynchronous operation and continue executing other code while the operation is in progress, preventing blocking and improving responsiveness.

Optimizing the Front-end: React.js Performance

While the back-end often takes the blame for performance bottlenecks, the front-end also plays a significant role in delivering a smooth and responsive user experience. Slow rendering times, excessive DOM manipulations, and inefficient state management can all contribute to a sluggish front-end. Let's explore some strategies for optimizing our React.js front-end.

Virtual DOM and Reconciliation: React's Efficiency Engine

React's Virtual DOM and reconciliation process are key to its efficiency. The Virtual DOM is a lightweight representation of the actual DOM that React maintains in memory. When changes occur in our application's state or props, React updates the Virtual DOM first and then performs a "diffing" algorithm to compare the new Virtual DOM with the previous one, identifying the minimal set of changes that need to be applied to the actual DOM. This process, called reconciliation, minimizes direct manipulations of the actual DOM, resulting in faster updates and improved performance.

Think of a painter who wants to make a small change to a large painting. Instead of repainting the entire canvas, the painter identifies the specific area that needs to be changed and only repaints that area, saving time and effort.

Component Optimization: Minimizing Re-renders

React's reconciliation process is efficient, but excessive component re-renders can still impact performance. When a component's state or props change, React re-renders the component and its children. If we're not careful, even small changes can trigger unnecessary re-renders of large parts of our component tree, slowing down our application.

Some strategies for minimizing component re-renders include:

- **`shouldComponentUpdate` Lifecycle Method:** In class components, we can use the `shouldComponentUpdate` lifecycle method to prevent unnecessary re-renders. This method allows us to compare the previous props and state with the new props and state and return `false` if the component doesn't need to re-render.

- **`React.memo` Higher-Order Component:** The `React.memo` higher-order component (HOC) memoizes the rendered output of a functional component based on its props. If the props haven't changed, React will reuse the memoized output, preventing unnecessary re-renders.

- **`useMemo` Hook:** The `useMemo` Hook memoizes the result of a function based on its dependencies. If the dependencies haven't changed, React will reuse the memoized result, preventing unnecessary re-computations.

Code Splitting: Loading What's Needed, When It's Needed

In large applications, loading the entire application code upfront can significantly increase the initial loading time, leading to a poor user experience. Code splitting is a technique that allows us to split our application code into smaller chunks that can be loaded on demand, reducing the initial loading time and improving performance.

Imagine a large library with thousands of books. Instead of building a single, massive building to house all the books, the library could be divided into smaller sections, each with its own collection of books. Visitors can then go directly to the section they're interested in, reducing the time it takes to find the books they need.

In React, we can use tools like Webpack or Parcel to implement code splitting. These tools allow us to split our code based on routes, components, or other criteria, loading only the necessary code when it's needed.

Lazy Loading: Deferring Non-Critical Resources

Lazy loading is a technique that defers the loading of non-critical resources, such as images or videos, until they are needed, improving the initial loading time and overall performance.

Imagine a long article with multiple images. Instead of loading all the images upfront, we can lazy load them, meaning the images will only be loaded when they are about to enter the user's viewport, reducing the initial loading time and improving the perceived performance of the article.

In React, we can use the `React.lazy` function to lazy load components, and we can use libraries like `react-lazyload` or `react-intersection-observer` to lazy load images or other resources.

Image Optimization: Reducing File Sizes

Images are often a major contributor to page size, and large image files can significantly impact loading times. Optimizing images by reducing their file sizes without compromising quality is an important step in improving front-end performance.

Some strategies for image optimization include:

- **Choose the Right Format:** Choose the right image format (JPEG, PNG, GIF, WebP) based on the image content and quality requirements.

- **Compress Images:** Use image compression tools, such as TinyPNG or ImageOptim, to reduce image file sizes without significant quality loss.

- **Use Responsive Images:** Serve different image sizes based on the user's screen size and resolution, ensuring that users don't download larger images than necessary.

Scalability: Handling Growth with Grace

Scalability refers to the ability of an application to handle increasing workloads, such as a growing number of users, requests, or data, without compromising performance or reliability. As our applications gain popularity and usage grows, scalability becomes a critical consideration to ensure that they can continue to meet the demands of their users.

Think of a bridge that's designed to handle a certain amount of traffic. As the city grows and traffic increases, the bridge might become congested, leading to delays and frustration. To accommodate the growing traffic, the city might need to build additional lanes or even a new bridge.

Similarly, in MERN stack applications, we need to design and architect our applications to handle growth gracefully. This might involve scaling our servers, databases, or other infrastructure to accommodate the increasing workload.

Horizontal Scaling: Distributing the Load

Horizontal scaling involves adding more servers to distribute the workload, ensuring that no single server becomes overloaded. When a request arrives, a load balancer distributes it to one of the available servers, ensuring that the load is evenly spread across the servers.

Imagine a restaurant with a single waiter. As the number of customers increases, the waiter might become overwhelmed, leading to slow service and unhappy customers. To handle the increasing workload, the restaurant could hire more waiters, allowing them to serve more customers efficiently.

In MERN stack applications, we can implement horizontal scaling using cloud platforms, such as AWS, Azure, or Google Cloud. These platforms offer services like load balancers and auto-scaling groups that allow us to automatically add or remove servers based on demand, ensuring that our applications can handle traffic spikes without performance degradation.

Vertical Scaling: Increasing Server Resources

Vertical scaling involves increasing the resources of a single server, such as CPU, memory, or storage, to handle a larger workload. This can be a quick and easy way to scale our applications, but it has limitations, as there's a limit to how much we can scale a single server.

Imagine a single-lane road that becomes congested during rush hour. To alleviate the congestion, the city could widen the road, adding more lanes to accommodate the increased traffic. However, there's a limit to how wide the road can be, and at some point, the city might need to build a new road altogether.

In MERN stack applications, vertical scaling can be achieved by upgrading our server hardware or choosing a more powerful server from our hosting provider. However, it's important to consider the limitations of vertical scaling and explore horizontal scaling options if our applications require significant scalability.

Database Scaling: Handling Growing Data

As our applications grow, the amount of data they handle also increases, putting a strain on our database. Scaling our database is essential to ensure that it can continue to handle the growing data volume efficiently.

MongoDB offers various scaling options:

- **Sharding:** Sharding involves dividing the data across multiple servers, allowing us to scale horizontally and handle large datasets.

- **Replica Sets:** Replica sets provide redundancy and high availability by replicating the data across multiple servers.

- **Vertical Scaling:** Similar to vertical scaling for servers, we can vertically scale our MongoDB database by increasing its resources, such as memory or storage.

Load Balancing: Distributing Requests Efficiently

Load balancing is a technique that distributes incoming requests across multiple servers, ensuring that no single server becomes overloaded. A load balancer acts as a traffic cop, directing requests to the most available server, ensuring that all servers are utilized efficiently and the overall system remains responsive.

Imagine a highway with multiple lanes. A traffic jam in one lane doesn't necessarily mean the entire highway is blocked. Traffic can still flow smoothly in the other lanes. A load balancer acts like a traffic management system, directing traffic to the least congested lanes, ensuring smooth traffic flow.

Load balancers can be implemented using hardware or software. Cloud platforms offer load balancing services that can automatically distribute requests across multiple servers, providing high availability and scalability.

Performance Monitoring: Keeping an Eye on Vital Signs

Performance monitoring is crucial for identifying bottlenecks, tracking performance trends, and ensuring that our applications are running smoothly. It involves collecting data about various aspects of our application's performance, such as response times, database query times, server resource utilization, and error rates.

Think of a doctor monitoring a patient's vital signs. By tracking heart rate, blood pressure, and other metrics, the doctor can identify potential health issues and take corrective action.

Several tools and services are available for performance monitoring in MERN stack applications, including:

- **New Relic:** A comprehensive performance monitoring platform that provides insights into application performance, server health, and user experience.

- **Datadog:** Another popular performance monitoring platform that offers a wide range of integrations and customizable dashboards.

- **Prometheus:** An open-source monitoring system that's popular in cloud-native environments.

By regularly monitoring our application's performance, we can identify potential issues early, optimize performance bottlenecks, and ensure that our applications remain responsive and reliable as they scale.

Performance and Scalability: An Ongoing Journey

Performance optimization and scalability are ongoing processes that require continuous attention, monitoring, and adjustments. As your application grows, user behavior changes, and new technologies emerge, you'll need to adapt your strategies and techniques to ensure that your application remains performant and scalable.

Remember that there's no one-size-fits-all solution for performance optimization and scalability. The best approach for your application depends on its specific requirements, architecture, and usage patterns. By understanding the concepts, tools, and techniques we've explored in this chapter, you'll be well-equipped to embark on this ongoing journey of optimizing your MERN stack applications for performance and scalability, ensuring they deliver exceptional user experiences even as they grow and evolve.

Chapter Twenty-Three: Working with Real-Time Data Using Socket.io

Throughout this book, we've delved into the MERN stack, learning to craft powerful web applications that handle data, respond to user interactions, and even manage user authentication and authorization. We've built applications that excel at displaying information and processing requests, but what about scenarios where we need to deliver information in real time, as it happens? Imagine building a chat application, a live collaboration tool, or a real-time dashboard that displays constantly updating data. In these cases, the traditional request-response model, where the client initiates a request and the server responds, falls short. We need a mechanism that allows for continuous, bidirectional communication between the client and the server, pushing updates in real time without the client constantly polling for changes.

Fortunately, the world of web development offers a powerful solution to this challenge: Socket.io. Socket.io is a JavaScript library that enables real-time, bidirectional communication between web clients and servers. It provides a simple and elegant API for establishing persistent connections between clients and servers, allowing for data to flow seamlessly in both directions, creating the foundation for truly interactive and real-time web experiences.

Socket.io: Enabling Real-Time Communication

Socket.io simplifies the complexities of real-time communication, abstracting away the low-level details of websockets and other protocols, providing a high-level API that's easy to use and integrate into your MERN stack applications.

Imagine two people having a conversation over walkie-talkies. They can talk to each other instantaneously, without having to dial a number or wait for a connection to be established. Socket.io

332

provides a similar experience for web applications, allowing for real-time communication between clients and servers.

Websockets: The Foundation of Socket.io

At the heart of Socket.io lies the concept of websockets. Websockets are a communication protocol that provides full-duplex communication channels over a single TCP connection. Unlike the traditional HTTP protocol, which is based on a request-response model, websockets allow for continuous, bidirectional communication, making them ideal for real-time applications.

Think of a telephone conversation. Both parties can talk and listen at the same time, creating a natural and interactive flow of communication. Websockets provide a similar experience for web applications, allowing for real-time data exchange between clients and servers.

Socket.io's Abstractions: Simplifying Real-Time Communication

Socket.io builds upon websockets, providing additional abstractions and features that simplify real-time communication:

- **Fallback Mechanisms:** Socket.io automatically falls back to other transport mechanisms, such as long polling or AJAX, if websockets are not available, ensuring that real-time communication is possible even in older browsers or environments where websockets are not supported.

- **Event-Based Communication:** Socket.io uses an event-based communication model, allowing clients and servers to emit and listen for events, making it easy to build real-time features.

- **Rooms and Namespaces:** Socket.io provides the concept of rooms and namespaces, allowing you to group clients and manage communication between specific groups or channels.

- **Broadcasting:** Socket.io makes it easy to broadcast messages to multiple clients or specific groups of clients.

- **Error Handling:** Socket.io provides mechanisms for handling errors and disconnections, ensuring that your real-time applications are robust and reliable.

Building a Real-Time Chat Application with Socket.io

Let's put Socket.io into action by building a simple real-time chat application. Our application will allow users to join a chat room, send messages to other users in the room, and receive messages in real time.

1. Setting Up the Back-end

We'll start by setting up the back-end using Express.js and Socket.io. Open your terminal or command prompt, navigate to the root directory of your server project (`server` in our previous deployment example), and install the Socket.io library:

```
npm install socket.io
```

Now, modify your `index.js` file to integrate Socket.io:

```
const express = require('express');

const http = require('http');
```

```javascript
const socketIo = require('socket.io');


const app = express();

const server = http.createServer(app); // Create an HTTP server

const io = socketIo(server); // Attach Socket.io to the server


// Define a simple API endpoint

app.get('/api/message', (req, res) => {

  res.json({ message: 'Hello from the server!' });

});


// Handle Socket.io connections

io.on('connection', (socket) => {

  console.log('New client connected');


  // Handle chat messages

  socket.on('chat message', (msg) => {

    console.log('Message:', msg);
```

```javascript
    io.emit('chat message', msg); //
Broadcast the message to all clients

    });


    // Handle disconnections

    socket.on('disconnect', () => {

        console.log('Client disconnected');

    });

});


const PORT = process.env.PORT || 5000;


server.listen(PORT, () =>
console.log(`Server running on port
${PORT}`));
```

In this code:

- We import the `http` and `socketIo` libraries.

- We create an HTTP server using `http.createServer(app)`.

- We attach Socket.io to the server using `socketIo(server)`.

- We listen for the `connection` event on the Socket.io instance. This event is fired whenever a new client connects to the server.

- Inside the `connection` event handler, we:

- Log a message indicating that a new client has connected.

- Listen for the `chat message` event. This event is fired whenever a client sends a chat message.

- When a `chat message` event is received, we log the message and broadcast it to all connected clients using `io.emit('chat message', msg)`.

- Listen for the `disconnect` event. This event is fired whenever a client disconnects from the server.

- When a `disconnect` event is received, we log a message indicating that a client has disconnected.

- We start the server using `server.listen(PORT, ...)`.

2. Setting Up the Front-end

Now, let's set up the front-end using React.js and the Socket.io client library. Open your terminal or command prompt, navigate to the root directory of your React front-end project (`client` in our previous deployment example), and install the Socket.io client library:

```
npm install socket.io-client
```

Now, create a new component named `Chat` that will handle the chat functionality:

```
import React, { useState, useEffect, useRef
} from 'react';

import socketIOClient from 'socket.io-
client';


const ENDPOINT = 'http://localhost:5000'; //
Replace with your server's URL


function Chat() {

  const [messages, setMessages] =
useState([]);

  const [input, setInput] = useState('');

  const socketRef = useRef();


  useEffect(() => {

    // Connect to the Socket.io server

    socketRef.current =
socketIOClient(ENDPOINT);



    // Listen for chat messages
```

```
  socketRef.current.on('chat message',
(msg) => {

    setMessages((prevMessages) =>
[...prevMessages, msg]);

    });


    // Clean up the connection when the
component unmounts

    return () => {

      socketRef.current.disconnect();

    };

  }, []);


  const handleSubmit = (event) => {

    event.preventDefault();


    // Send the chat message

    socketRef.current.emit('chat message',
input);

    setInput('');

  };
```

```
return (
```

Chat Room

```
            {messages.map((message, index)
   => (



  • {message}


        ))}




   );

}
```

```
export default Chat;
```

In this code:

- We import the `socketIOClient` library.

- We define a constant `ENDPOINT` that specifies the URL of our Socket.io server. Replace `http://localhost:5000` with the actual URL of your server.

- We initialize three state variables: `messages` to store the chat messages, `input` to store the user's input, and `socketRef` to store a reference to the Socket.io socket.

- We use the `useEffect` Hook to:

- Connect to the Socket.io server using `socketIOClient(ENDPOINT)`.

- Listen for the `chat message` event. When a message is received, we add it to the `messages` array.

- Clean up the connection when the component unmounts by calling `socketRef.current.disconnect()`.

- The `handleSubmit` function sends the chat message to the server using `socketRef.current.emit('chat message', input)`.

- We render a list of chat messages and a form for sending messages.

3. Integrating the Chat Component

Finally, let's integrate the Chat component into our App component:

```
import React from 'react';

import Chat from './Chat';


function App() {

    return (




    );

}


export default App;
```

4. Running the Application

Save all the files and start your development server. Open two browser windows and navigate to http://localhost:3000.

343

You should now be able to send messages between the two browser windows in real time.

Rooms and Namespaces: Organizing Communication

In our chat application, all connected clients receive all messages. In real-world applications, we often need to organize communication into separate channels or groups, allowing users to communicate only with specific users or groups. Socket.io provides the concept of rooms and namespaces to achieve this.

Rooms: Grouping Clients

Rooms allow you to group clients and broadcast messages to specific groups. When a client connects to a room, it will only receive messages that are sent to that room.

To join a room, you use the `socket.join(roomName)` method. To leave a room, you use the `socket.leave(roomName)` method.

To broadcast a message to a specific room, you use the `io.to(roomName).emit(eventName, data)` method.

Let's modify our chat application to allow users to join different rooms:

Server-side (index.js):

```
// ... (other code)



io.on('connection', (socket) => {

  // ... (other event handlers)
```

```javascript
// Handle joining rooms

socket.on('join room', (roomName) => {

    socket.join(roomName);

    console.log(`Client joined room:
${roomName}`);

});


// Handle leaving rooms

socket.on('leave room', (roomName) => {

    socket.leave(roomName);

    console.log(`Client left room:
${roomName}`);

});


// Handle chat messages

socket.on('chat message', (msg, roomName)
=> {

    console.log('Message:', msg, 'Room:',
roomName);

    io.to(roomName).emit('chat message',
msg); // Broadcast to the specific room
```

```
  });


  // ... (other event handlers)
});


// ... (other code)
```

Client-side (Chat.js):

```
// ... (other code)


function Chat() {
  // ... (other state variables)

  const [roomName, setRoomName] =
useState('');


  // ... (other code)


  const handleJoinRoom = () => {
```

```
    socketRef.current.emit('join room',
roomName);

  };


  const handleLeaveRoom = () => {

    socketRef.current.emit('leave room',
roomName);

  };


  const handleSubmit = (event) => {

    event.preventDefault();


    // Send the chat message to the specific
room

    socketRef.current.emit('chat message',
input, roomName);

    setInput('');

  };


  return (
```

Chat Rooms

```
        {roomName}
setRoomName(event.target.value)}
```

```
        />
```

```
        Join Room
```

```
        Leave Room
```

```
    {/* ... (rest of the component) */}
```

```
  );
```

```
}
```

```
// ... (other code)
```

Now, users can enter a room name and join or leave specific rooms. Messages will only be broadcast to users in the same room.

Namespaces: Organizing Communication by Feature

Namespaces allow you to organize communication by feature or functionality. You can create separate namespaces for different features of your application, such as chat, notifications, or real-time updates.

To create a namespace, you use the `io.of(namespaceName)` method. Each namespace has its own event handlers and connection management.

Let's create a separate namespace for notifications:

Server-side (index.js):

```
// ... (other code)
```

```
const notificationNamespace =
io.of('/notifications');
```

```
notificationNamespace.on('connection',
(socket) => {
```

```
  console.log('New client connected to
notifications namespace');


  // Handle notification events

  socket.on('send notification',
(notification) => {

    console.log('Notification:',
notification);

    notificationNamespace.emit('receive
notification', notification);

  });


  // ... (other event handlers)
});


// ... (other code)
```

Client-side (Notifications.js):

```
import React, { useState, useEffect, useRef
} from 'react';
```

```javascript
import socketIOClient from 'socket.io-
client';


const ENDPOINT = 'http://localhost:5000'; //
Replace with your server's URL


function Notifications() {

  const [notifications, setNotifications] =
useState([]);

  const socketRef = useRef();


  useEffect(() => {

    // Connect to the notifications
namespace

    socketRef.current =
socketIOClient(`${ENDPOINT}/notifications`);


    // Listen for notifications

    socketRef.current.on('receive
notification', (notification) => {

      setNotifications((prevNotifications)
=> [

        ...prevNotifications,
```

```
        notification,

    ]);

  });


    // Clean up the connection when the
component unmounts

    return () => {

      socketRef.current.disconnect();

    };

  }, []);


    return (
```

Notifications

```
{notifications.map((notification,
index) => (


    • {notification}


        ))}
```

```
  );

}
```

```
export default Notifications;
```

Now, we have a separate namespace for notifications, allowing us to organize communication by feature.

Scaling Socket.io: Handling a Growing Audience

As your real-time application gains popularity and the number of connected clients increases, scalability becomes a crucial consideration. Socket.io is designed to be scalable, but you might need to implement additional strategies to handle a large number of connections efficiently.

Load Balancing: Distributing Connections

Load balancing is a technique that distributes incoming connections across multiple servers, ensuring that no single server becomes overloaded. A load balancer acts as a traffic cop, directing connections to the most available server, ensuring that all servers are utilized efficiently and the overall system remains responsive.

Imagine a highway with multiple lanes. A traffic jam in one lane doesn't necessarily mean the entire highway is blocked. Traffic can still flow smoothly in the other lanes. A load balancer acts like a traffic management system, directing traffic to the least congested lanes, ensuring smooth traffic flow.

Socket.io supports load balancing through the use of Redis or other message brokers. These brokers act as intermediaries between the Socket.io servers and the clients, distributing messages and connections across multiple servers.

Horizontal Scaling: Adding More Servers

Horizontal scaling involves adding more servers to handle the increasing workload. When a new client connects, the load balancer directs it to one of the available servers, ensuring that the load is evenly spread across the servers.

Imagine a restaurant with a single waiter. As the number of customers increases, the waiter might become overwhelmed, leading to slow service and unhappy customers. To handle the increasing workload, the restaurant could hire more waiters, allowing them to serve more customers efficiently.

Cloud platforms, such as AWS, Azure, or Google Cloud, make it easy to implement horizontal scaling. They offer services like load balancers and auto-scaling groups that allow you to automatically add or remove servers based on demand, ensuring that your application can handle traffic spikes without performance degradation.

Using a CDN: Caching Static Assets

A Content Delivery Network (CDN) is a network of servers distributed around the world that cache static assets, such as images, CSS files, and JavaScript files, closer to users. When a user requests a static asset, the CDN serves it from the closest server, reducing latency and improving loading times.

Imagine a library with branches in multiple cities. If you want to borrow a book that's available in a branch near you, you don't have to travel to the main library. You can simply visit the nearest branch, reducing the time and effort required to access the book.

Using a CDN for your Socket.io application can improve performance by caching static assets closer to users, reducing the load on your servers and improving the overall user experience.

Socket.io: Expanding the Possibilities of Web Applications

Socket.io empowers us to build truly interactive and real-time web applications, pushing the boundaries of what's possible with traditional web technologies. Its bidirectional communication capabilities, event-based model, and scalability features allow us to create applications that respond to events as they happen, delivering information in real-time and creating engaging user experiences.

As you explore the world of real-time web development, remember that Socket.io is just one piece of the puzzle. Building robust and scalable real-time applications requires careful consideration of various factors, including server architecture, database design, and front-end optimization.

Chapter Twenty-Four: Building a Serverless MERN Stack Application

In our exploration of the MERN stack, we've traversed a fascinating landscape of technologies, architectures, and techniques for building robust and dynamic web applications. We've learned to craft powerful back-ends, engaging front-ends, manage state efficiently, interact with databases, secure our applications, and even test them rigorously. Throughout this journey, we've often relied on traditional server-based architectures, where our applications reside on servers that we manage and maintain. However, the world of web development is constantly evolving, and new paradigms, such as serverless computing, are revolutionizing the way we build and deploy applications. In this chapter, we'll delve into the realm of serverless computing and explore how we can leverage its power to build serverless MERN stack applications. We'll discover the benefits of serverless, learn about popular serverless platforms, and walk through the process of building and deploying a serverless MERN application, embracing a new era of web development where we can focus on building great applications without the burden of server management.

Serverless Computing: Shifting the Paradigm

Serverless computing is a cloud computing execution model where the cloud provider dynamically manages the allocation of machine resources. Pricing is based on the actual amount of resources consumed by an application, rather than on pre-purchased units of capacity. It signifies a paradigm shift where developers can focus on writing code without worrying about the underlying infrastructure. The cloud provider takes care of provisioning, scaling, and managing the servers, allowing developers to concentrate on building and deploying their applications.

Imagine ordering food at a restaurant. You don't need to worry about the kitchen staff, the ovens, or the dishes. You simply place your order, and the restaurant takes care of preparing and serving your meal. Serverless computing provides a similar experience for developers. You write your code, deploy it to the serverless platform, and the platform takes care of executing it, scaling it based on demand, and managing the underlying resources.

The Allure of Serverless: Benefits and Considerations

Serverless computing offers a compelling set of benefits, making it an increasingly popular choice for building modern web applications:

- **Reduced Operational Overhead:** Serverless eliminates the need for server management, freeing developers from tasks like provisioning, scaling, patching, and monitoring servers. The cloud provider handles all the infrastructure management, allowing developers to focus on writing code.

- **Scalability and Elasticity:** Serverless platforms automatically scale your application's resources based on demand. If your application experiences a sudden surge in traffic, the platform will automatically provision more resources to handle the load. Conversely, if traffic decreases, the platform will scale down the resources, ensuring that you only pay for what you use.

- **Cost-Effectiveness:** Serverless computing can be very cost-effective, especially for applications with variable workloads or infrequent usage. You only pay for the actual execution time of your code, not for idle server time.

- **Faster Development Cycles:** Serverless computing allows for faster development cycles, as developers can focus on writing code and deploying it quickly without worrying about infrastructure setup.

However, serverless computing also comes with considerations:

- **Vendor Lock-in:** Using a serverless platform can create vendor lock-in, making it more difficult to switch to a different platform in the future.

- **Cold Starts:** Serverless functions might experience cold starts, where the platform needs to initialize the function before it can execute, leading to a slight delay in the initial response time.

- **Statelessness:** Serverless functions are typically stateless, meaning they don't retain any state between invocations. This requires careful consideration for applications that need to maintain state.

Serverless Platforms: The Power of Cloud Computing

Several cloud providers offer serverless computing platforms, each with its unique features, strengths, and pricing models. Some popular serverless platforms include:

AWS Lambda: The Pioneer of Serverless

AWS Lambda is a serverless compute service that lets you run code without provisioning or managing servers. You upload your code, and Lambda takes care of everything required to run and scale your code with high availability. You can set up your code to automatically trigger from other AWS services or call it directly from any web or mobile app.

Azure Functions: Serverless on the Microsoft Cloud

Azure Functions is a serverless compute service that enables you to run event-triggered code without having to explicitly provision or manage infrastructure. Azure Functions can be triggered by a variety of events, including HTTP requests, timer triggers, messages from queues, and more.

Google Cloud Functions: Google's Serverless Offering

Google Cloud Functions is a serverless execution environment for building and connecting cloud services. With Cloud Functions, you write simple, single-purpose functions that are attached to events emitted from your cloud infrastructure and services. Your function is triggered when an event being watched is fired. Your code executes in a fully managed environment.

Building a Serverless To-Do List Application

Let's put serverless computing into practice by building a simple serverless to-do list application. Our application will allow users to add, delete, and view their to-do items. We'll use AWS Lambda for our serverless functions, MongoDB Atlas for our database, and React.js for our front-end.

1. Setting Up MongoDB Atlas

We'll start by setting up our MongoDB database using MongoDB Atlas, a cloud-based database service offered by MongoDB. MongoDB Atlas provides a managed MongoDB instance, eliminating the need for manual installation and configuration.

- **Create a MongoDB Atlas Account:** If you don't already have one, create a free MongoDB Atlas account at https://www.mongodb.com/cloud/atlas.

- **Create a Cluster:** Follow the instructions in the MongoDB Atlas documentation to create a new cluster. Choose a free tier cluster for this demonstration.

- **Create a Database and Collection:** Create a new database named "serverless-todo" and a new collection named "todos."

- **Get Your Connection String:** From the MongoDB Atlas dashboard, get the connection string for your cluster. You'll need this connection string to connect to your database from your serverless functions.

2. Setting Up AWS Lambda

Now, let's set up our serverless functions using AWS Lambda.

- **Create an AWS Account:** If you don't already have one, create an AWS account at https://aws.amazon.com.

- **Navigate to the Lambda Console:** From the AWS Management Console, navigate to the Lambda service.

- **Create a New Function:** Click "Create function" to create a new Lambda function.

- **Choose Author from Scratch:** Select "Author from scratch" as the function creation method.

- **Configure Function:** Configure the function as follows:

- **Function name:** `createTodo` (We'll create separate functions for each operation.)

- **Runtime:** `Node.js 14.x` (Choose the latest Node.js runtime.)

- **Architecture:** `x86_64` (Choose the architecture that matches your system.)

- **Permissions:** Create a new role with basic Lambda permissions.

- **Click "Create function."**

3. Writing the Create To-Do Function

Now that we have our Lambda function created, let's write the code to create a new to-do item. Replace the default code in the function's code editor with the following code:

```javascript
const { MongoClient } = require('mongodb');

const uri = 'your-mongodb-connection-string'; // Replace with your MongoDB connection string

const client = new MongoClient(uri, {
  useNewUrlParser: true,
  useUnifiedTopology: true,
});

exports.handler = async (event) => {
  try {
    await client.connect();

    const database = client.db('serverless-todo'); // Replace with your database name

    const collection = database.collection('todos'); // Replace with your collection name

    const { todo } = JSON.parse(event.body); // Get the to-do text from the request body
```

```javascript
    const result = await
collection.insertOne({ todo, completed:
false });


    return {

      statusCode: 201,

      body: JSON.stringify({ message: 'To-do
created successfully', id: result.insertedId
}),

    };

  } catch (error) {

    console.error('Error creating to-do:',
error);


    return {

      statusCode: 500,

      body: JSON.stringify({ message: 'Error
creating to-do' }),

    };

  } finally {

    await client.close();

  }
```

```
};
```

In this code:

- We import the `MongoClient` class from the `mongodb` library.

- We define the `uri` variable, which should contain your MongoDB connection string. Replace `'your-mongodb-connection-string'` with the connection string you obtained from MongoDB Atlas.

- We create a new `MongoClient` instance using the `uri` and connection options.

- The `exports.handler` function is the entry point for our Lambda function. It receives an `event` object that contains information about the invocation, including the request body.

- We parse the to-do text from the request body using `JSON.parse(event.body)`.

- We connect to the MongoDB database using `client.connect()`.

- We get references to the database and collection using `client.db('serverless-todo')` and `database.collection('todos')`, respectively. Replace `'serverless-todo'` and `'todos'` with your actual database and collection names.

- We insert a new to-do document into the collection using `collection.insertOne()`.

- We return a success response with a 201 (Created) status code and the ID of the newly created to-do item.

- We handle any errors that occur during the process and return an error response with a 500 (Internal Server Error) status code.

- We close the MongoDB connection using `client.close()` in the `finally` block.

4. Testing the Create To-Do Function

Now that we have our create to-do function written, let's test it out.

- **Deploy the Function:** From the Lambda console, click "Deploy" to deploy the function.

- **Test the Function:** Click "Test" to open the test event configuration.

- **Configure Test Event:** Choose "Create new event" and name it "CreateTodoEvent." In the event JSON, replace the default content with the following:

```
{

    "body": "{\"todo\": \"Buy groceries\"}"

}
```

- **Click "Create."**

- **Run the Test:** Click "Test" to run the test event. You should see a successful response with a 201 status code and the ID of the newly created to-do item.

5. Writing the Get To-Dos Function

Let's create another Lambda function to retrieve the to-do items.

- **Create a New Function:** From the Lambda console, click "Create function" to create a new Lambda function.

- **Configure Function:** Configure the function as follows:

- **Function name:** `getTodos`

- **Runtime:** `Node.js 14.x`

- **Architecture:** `x86_64`

- **Permissions:** Use the same role you created for the `createTodo` function.

- **Click "Create function."**

Replace the default code in the function's code editor with the following code:

```
const { MongoClient } = require('mongodb');
```

```
const uri = 'your-mongodb-connection-string'; // Replace with your MongoDB connection string
```

```javascript
const client = new MongoClient(uri, {

  useNewUrlParser: true,

  useUnifiedTopology: true,

});


exports.handler = async (event) => {

  try {

    await client.connect();

    const database = client.db('serverless-todo'); // Replace with your database name

    const collection = database.collection('todos'); // Replace with your collection name


    const result = await collection.find({}).toArray();


    return {

      statusCode: 200,

      body: JSON.stringify(result),

    };

  } catch (error) {
```

```
    console.error('Error retrieving to-
dos:', error);


    return {

      statusCode: 500,

      body: JSON.stringify({ message: 'Error
retrieving to-dos' }),

    };

  } finally {

    await client.close();

  }

};
```

In this code:

- We use `collection.find({})` to retrieve all to-do documents from the collection.

- We convert the result to an array using `toArray()`.

- We return a success response with a 200 (OK) status code and the array of to-do items.

6. Testing the Get To-Dos Function

- **Deploy the Function:** From the Lambda console, click "Deploy" to deploy the function.

- **Test the Function:** Click "Test" to open the test event configuration.

- **Configure Test Event:** Choose "Create new event" and name it "GetTodosEvent." Use the default event JSON.

- **Click "Create."**

- **Run the Test:** Click "Test" to run the test event. You should see a successful response with a 200 status code and an array of to-do items, which might be empty if you haven't created any to-dos yet.

7. Writing the Delete To-Do Function

Let's create another Lambda function to delete a to-do item.

- **Create a New Function:** From the Lambda console, click "Create function" to create a new Lambda function.

- **Configure Function:** Configure the function as follows:

- **Function name:** `deleteTodo`

- **Runtime:** `Node.js 14.x`

- **Architecture:** `x86_64`

- **Permissions:** Use the same role you created for the previous functions.

- **Click "Create function."**

Replace the default code in the function's code editor with the following code:

```
const { MongoClient, ObjectId } =
require('mongodb');


const uri = 'your-mongodb-connection-
string'; // Replace with your MongoDB
connection string


const client = new MongoClient(uri, {

  useNewUrlParser: true,

  useUnifiedTopology: true,

});


exports.handler = async (event) => {

  try {

    await client.connect();

    const database = client.db('serverless-
todo'); // Replace with your database name

    const collection =
database.collection('todos'); // Replace
with your collection name
```

```javascript
    const { id } = event.pathParameters; //
Get the to-do ID from the path parameters


    const result = await
collection.deleteOne({ _id: new ObjectId(id)
});


    if (result.deletedCount === 1) {

      return {

        statusCode: 200,

        body: JSON.stringify({ message: 'To-
do deleted successfully' }),

      };

    } else {

      return {

        statusCode: 404,

        body: JSON.stringify({ message: 'To-
do not found' }),

      };

    }

  } catch (error) {

    console.error('Error deleting to-do:',
error);
```

```
    return {

      statusCode: 500,

      body: JSON.stringify({ message: 'Error
deleting to-do' }),

    };

  } finally {

    await client.close();

  }

};
```

In this code:

- We import the `ObjectId` class from the `mongodb` library.

- We get the to-do ID from the `event.pathParameters` object.

- We use `collection.deleteOne({ _id: new ObjectId(id) })` to delete the to-do document with the specified ID.

- We check if the `deletedCount` is 1, indicating that a to-do was deleted. If so, we return a success response. Otherwise, we return a 404 (Not Found) response.

8. Testing the Delete To-Do Function

- **Deploy the Function:** From the Lambda console, click "Deploy" to deploy the function.

- **Test the Function:** Click "Test" to open the test event configuration.

- **Configure Test Event:** Choose "Create new event" and name it "DeleteTodoEvent." In the event JSON, replace the default content with the following, replacing `your-todo-id` with the ID of a to-do item you want to delete:

```
{

    "pathParameters": {

        "id": "your-todo-id"

    }

}
```

- **Click "Create."**

- **Run the Test:** Click "Test" to run the test event. You should see a successful response with a 200 status code if the to-do was deleted successfully or a 404 status code if the to-do was not found.

9. Creating API Gateway Endpoints

We've created our Lambda functions, but we need a way to expose them as API endpoints so that our React front-end can interact with them. AWS API Gateway provides a service for creating and managing API endpoints that can trigger our Lambda functions.

- **Navigate to the API Gateway Console:** From the AWS Management Console, navigate to the API Gateway service.

- **Create a New API:** Click "Create API" to create a new API.

- **Choose REST API:** Select "REST API" as the API type.

- **Configure API:** Configure the API as follows:

- **API name:** `serverless-todo-api`

- **Endpoint Type:** `Regional`

- **Click "Create API."**

10. Creating API Resources and Methods

Now, let's create API resources and methods for our to-do operations:

- **Create a Resource:** Under "Resources," click "Actions" and select "Create Resource."

- **Resource Name:** `todos`

- **Resource Path:** `/todos`

- **Click "Create Resource."**

- **Create a POST Method:** Under the `todos` resource, click "Actions" and select "Create Method."

- **Choose POST from the dropdown.**

- **Integration Type:** `Lambda Function`

- **Lambda Function:** Choose the `createTodo` function from your region.

- **Click "Save."**

- **Deploy the API:** Click "Actions" and select "Deploy API." Choose a new deployment stage (e.g., "prod") and click "Deploy."

- **Repeat the above steps to create GET and DELETE methods for the todos resource, associating them with the getTodos and deleteTodo functions, respectively.**

- **For the DELETE method, create a child resource named {id} with a path parameter id and associate it with the deleteTodo function.**

After deploying the API, you'll get a base URL for your API. Note this URL, as you'll need it for your React front-end.

11. Building the React Front-end

Now, let's build the React front-end for our to-do list application. Open your terminal or command prompt, navigate to the root directory of your React front-end project (`client` in our previous deployment example), and create a new component named `TodoList`:

```
import React, { useState, useEffect } from
'react';
```

```javascript
import axios from 'axios';


const API_BASE_URL = 'your-api-gateway-base-
url'; // Replace with your API Gateway base
URL


function TodoList() {

  const [todos, setTodos] = useState([]);

  const [newTodo, setNewTodo] =
useState('');


  useEffect(() => {

    const fetchTodos = async () => {

      try {

        const response = await
axios.get(`${API_BASE_URL}/todos`);

        setTodos(response.data);

      } catch (error) {

        console.error('Error fetching to-
dos:', error);

      }

    };
```

```
    fetchTodos();

  }, []);


  const handleAddTodo = async () => {

    try {

      const response = await
axios.post(`${API_BASE_URL}/todos`, {

        todo: newTodo,

      });

      setTodos((prevTodos) => [...prevTodos,
response.data]);

      setNewTodo('');

    } catch (error) {

      console.error('Error adding to-do:',
error);

    }

  };


  const handleDeleteTodo = async (id) => {

    try {
```

```
      await
axios.delete(`${API_BASE_URL}/todos/${id}`);

      setTodos((prevTodos) =>
prevTodos.filter((todo) => todo._id !==
id));

    } catch (error) {

      console.error('Error deleting to-do:',
error);

    }

  };


  return (
```

To-Do List

{newTodo}
```
setNewTodo(event.target.value)}
```

```
/>
```

Add

```
{todos.map((todo) => (
```

•

```
{todo.todo}
```

```
                handleDeleteTodo(todo._id)}>

                        Delete




            ))}




    );

}



export default TodoList;
```

In this code:

- We define the `API_BASE_URL` constant, which should contain the base URL of your API Gateway endpoint. Replace `'your-api-gateway-base-url'` with the actual base URL.

- We use `axios` to make GET, POST, and DELETE requests to our API endpoints.

- The `handleAddTodo` function sends a POST request to create a new to-do item.

- The `handleDeleteTodo` function sends a DELETE request to delete a to-do item.

12. Integrating the TodoList Component

Finally, integrate the `TodoList` component into your `App` component:

```
import React from 'react';

import TodoList from './TodoList';


function App() {

  return (




  );

}


export default App;
```

13. Running the Application

Save all the files and start your development server. You should now see a to-do list application where you can add, delete, and view your to-do items. The data is stored in your MongoDB Atlas database, and the operations are handled by your serverless functions on AWS Lambda.

Serverless: A New Era of Web Development

Serverless computing offers a paradigm shift in web development, allowing developers to focus on building applications without the burden of server management. Its scalability, cost-effectiveness, and faster development cycles make it a compelling choice for modern web applications. While serverless comes with its considerations, its benefits often outweigh the drawbacks, especially for applications with variable workloads or infrequent usage.

As you explore the world of serverless computing, remember that it's still a relatively new paradigm, and best practices are constantly evolving. Experiment with different serverless platforms, explore the vast ecosystem of serverless tools and services, and stay informed about the latest developments in this exciting and rapidly evolving space.

Chapter Twenty-Five: Best Practices and Future Trends in MERN Development

As you stand at the cusp of your MERN stack development journey, equipped with the knowledge and skills you've acquired throughout this book, it's essential to remember that the world of web development is a dynamic and ever-evolving landscape. Best practices change, new technologies emerge, and the quest for building exceptional web experiences is an ongoing endeavor. This chapter aims to provide you with a compass to navigate this evolving terrain, offering insights into best practices that will elevate the quality and maintainability of your MERN stack applications and a glimpse into the future trends that are shaping the horizon of web development.

Best Practices: The Pillars of Quality and Maintainability

Building high-quality, maintainable MERN stack applications requires adhering to best practices that ensure code clarity, organization, efficiency, and scalability. These best practices encompass various aspects of the development process, from code style and architecture to testing and deployment.

Code Style and Organization: The Art of Readable Code

Code is read more often than it's written. Writing clean, readable, and well-organized code is essential for collaboration, maintainability, and reducing the cognitive load for anyone who needs to understand or modify the code, including your future self.

Imagine a library where the books are randomly arranged on shelves, without any categorization or order. Finding a specific book would be a daunting and frustrating task. Similarly, poorly organized and unreadable code can make it difficult to understand the application's logic, debug issues, or add new features.

Some best practices for code style and organization in MERN stack applications include:

- **Consistent Indentation and Spacing:** Use a consistent indentation style (spaces or tabs) and spacing around operators and keywords to improve readability.

- **Meaningful Variable and Function Names:** Choose descriptive and meaningful names for your variables, functions, and components, conveying their purpose and functionality clearly.

- **Modular Code:** Break down your code into smaller, reusable modules or components, each responsible for a specific task or feature. This promotes code reusability, reduces complexity, and makes it easier to test and maintain your application.

- **Comments and Documentation:** Write clear and concise comments to explain your code's logic, purpose, and any non-obvious decisions. Consider using tools like JSDoc to generate documentation from your comments, making it easier for others to understand your code.

- **Code Linting:** Use a code linter, such as ESLint, to enforce code style rules and identify potential errors or code quality issues. Linters help you maintain consistency and adherence to best practices.

Project Structure: Organizing Your MERN Stack Components

A well-organized project structure is crucial for managing the different parts of your MERN stack application, especially as your application grows in size and complexity. A logical and consistent project structure makes it easier to find files, understand the application's organization, and collaborate with other developers.

Imagine a well-organized workshop where tools and materials are neatly arranged in labeled drawers and cabinets. Finding the right tool or material is quick and efficient. Similarly, a well-structured project makes it easier to navigate the codebase, find the components or modules you need, and understand how the different parts of the application fit together.

There are various approaches to structuring MERN stack applications, and the best approach often depends on the specific needs of your project. However, some common patterns include:

- **Feature-Based Structure:** Organize your code based on features or functionalities. Create separate folders for each feature, containing all the components, modules, and tests related to that feature.

- **Component-Based Structure:** Organize your code based on components. Create separate folders for each type of component, such as pages, containers, or presentational components.

- **Layer-Based Structure:** Organize your code based on layers or tiers, such as the front-end (React), back-end (Express.js and MongoDB), and shared modules.

Regardless of the chosen structure, ensure consistency, clear naming conventions, and a logical hierarchy that reflects the application's organization.

State Management: Taming the Data Flow

State management is a critical aspect of building complex React applications. As your application grows, the data flow between components can become intricate and difficult to manage, potentially leading to bugs, performance issues, and a frustrating development experience. Choosing the right state management solution for your application is crucial to maintain data consistency, predictability, and ease of development.

Imagine a large orchestra with multiple musicians playing different instruments. Without a conductor to coordinate their actions, the music would be chaotic and dissonant. State management solutions act as the conductor, orchestrating the data flow between components, ensuring harmony and consistency.

We've explored Redux, a popular state management library, in previous chapters. Redux provides a centralized store, a predictable data flow, and powerful tools for managing complex state. However, other state management solutions are available, each with its strengths and weaknesses:

- **Context API:** React's built-in Context API provides a way to share data between components without prop drilling. It's suitable for simple state management scenarios, but it can become cumbersome for managing complex state.

- **MobX:** MobX is a state management library that emphasizes simplicity and reactivity. It uses observables and reactions to automatically update components when the state changes.

- **Zustand:** Zustand is a lightweight and minimal state management library that's easy to learn and use. It's suitable for small to medium-sized applications.

The choice of a state management solution depends on factors such as the complexity of your application, your team's experience, and your personal preferences. Evaluate the different options and choose the solution that best suits your needs.

Data Fetching: Handling Asynchronous Operations

Fetching data from APIs is a common requirement in MERN stack applications. Asynchronous operations, such as fetching data, can introduce complexity and potential race conditions if not handled carefully. Ensuring efficient and reliable data fetching is crucial for delivering a smooth user experience and maintaining data consistency.

Imagine a restaurant kitchen receiving multiple orders simultaneously. The chefs need to coordinate their actions to ensure that each order is prepared correctly and delivered on time, avoiding confusion and delays. Data fetching mechanisms act as the kitchen staff, coordinating asynchronous operations, handling responses, and updating the application's state accordingly.

We've explored Axios, a popular HTTP client library, in previous chapters. Axios provides a convenient and efficient way to make HTTP requests, handle responses, and manage errors. Other data fetching libraries and techniques are available:

- **Fetch API:** JavaScript's built-in Fetch API provides a more modern approach to making HTTP requests compared to traditional XMLHttpRequest.

- **GraphQL:** GraphQL is a query language for APIs and a runtime for fulfilling those queries with your existing data. It allows clients to request exactly the data they need, reducing over-fetching and improving performance.

- **SWR:** SWR is a React Hooks library for data fetching that provides features like caching, revalidation, and focus revalidation.

- **React Query:** React Query is another React Hooks library for data fetching that offers similar features to SWR, along with features like pagination and infinite loading.

Choose the data fetching library or technique that best aligns with your application's needs and architecture.

Routing: Navigating the Application

Routing is a fundamental aspect of web applications, allowing users to navigate between different views or pages. Defining clear and logical routes, handling navigation events, and managing route parameters are essential for creating a user-friendly and intuitive application.

Imagine a well-designed city with clearly marked roads and signs, guiding drivers to their destinations efficiently. Routing mechanisms act as the city planners, defining the paths within your application, guiding users to the right components or views based on the URL.

We've explored React Router, a popular routing library for React, in previous chapters. React Router provides a declarative way to define routes, handle navigation, and manage route parameters. Other routing libraries and techniques are available:

- **Next.js:** Next.js is a React framework that provides built-in routing, automatic code splitting, server-side rendering, and other features for building performant and SEO-friendly applications.

- **Gatsby:** Gatsby is another React framework that focuses on static site generation, providing a fast and efficient way to build websites and applications.

- **Reach Router:** Reach Router is a routing library that emphasizes accessibility and performance.

Choose the routing library or technique that aligns with your application's requirements and complexity.

Authentication and Authorization: Securing Your Application

Security is a paramount concern in web applications, especially those handling sensitive user data. Implementing robust authentication and authorization mechanisms is crucial for verifying user identities, protecting sensitive information, and ensuring that users can only access the resources they are authorized to access.

Imagine a secure building with multiple levels of access control, such as key cards, security guards, and biometric scanners, ensuring that only authorized individuals can enter specific areas. Authentication and authorization mechanisms act as the security systems, verifying identities, granting permissions, and protecting sensitive data.

We've explored JWT (JSON Web Token) authentication and role-based access control in previous chapters. JWT provides a stateless and secure way to authenticate users, while role-based access control allows you to define roles and permissions to restrict access to specific resources or actions. Other authentication and authorization techniques are available:

- **OAuth 2.0:** OAuth 2.0 is an industry-standard protocol for authorization that allows users to grant third-party applications access to their resources without sharing their passwords.

- **OpenID Connect (OIDC):** OIDC is an authentication layer built on top of OAuth 2.0 that provides a standardized way to verify user identities.

- **Passport.js:** Passport.js is an authentication middleware for Node.js that supports various authentication strategies, including local authentication, OAuth, and OpenID Connect.

Choose the authentication and authorization techniques that align with your application's security requirements and the level of sensitivity of the data it handles.

Error Handling: Graceful Recovery from Failures

Errors are an inevitable part of software development. Handling errors gracefully, providing informative error messages, and preventing application crashes are essential for a positive user experience and maintaining the integrity of your application.

Imagine a well-designed airplane with multiple backup systems and safety procedures, ensuring that even in the event of a system failure, the plane can land safely. Error handling mechanisms act as the backup systems, catching errors, preventing crashes, and guiding the application towards a safe recovery.

Error handling in MERN stack applications involves handling errors at various levels:

- **Front-End Error Handling:** Catching errors in React components, displaying user-friendly error messages, and preventing the application from crashing due to front-end errors.

- **Back-End Error Handling:** Handling errors in Express.js routes, logging errors, returning appropriate error responses to the client, and preventing the server from crashing due to back-end errors.

- **Database Error Handling:** Handling errors during database interactions, retrying failed operations, and ensuring data consistency.

- **Centralized Error Logging:** Implementing centralized error logging using services like Sentry or Rollbar to track errors, identify trends, and facilitate debugging.

Implement error handling mechanisms at each layer of your application to ensure graceful recovery from failures, maintain data integrity, and provide a positive user experience even in the face of unexpected events.

Testing: Ensuring Reliability and Correctness

Testing is an integral part of building reliable and high-quality MERN stack applications. It involves writing code that executes different parts of your application and verifies that they behave as expected. Testing helps you catch bugs early, prevent regressions, and maintain a high level of code quality.

Imagine a bridge undergoing rigorous stress testing to ensure its structural integrity. Testing your application is like stress-testing your code, identifying weaknesses and vulnerabilities, and ensuring that it can handle the expected workload.

We've explored different types of tests, including unit tests, integration tests, and end-to-end tests, in previous chapters. Different types of tests focus on different aspects of the application and provide varying levels of coverage.

Some best practices for testing MERN stack applications include:

- **Write Tests for All Critical Features:** Ensure that all critical features of your application are covered by tests.

- **Focus on User Interactions:** When testing React components, focus on how the component interacts with the user, simulating real user interactions and verifying that the component behaves as expected.

- **Use Mocking to Isolate Units of Code:** Use mocking to replace dependencies with mock objects, allowing you to test units of code in isolation, avoiding complex setup and ensuring that your tests are focused and efficient.

- **Integrate Testing into Your Workflow:** Integrate testing into your development workflow, running tests automatically whenever code changes are made. Consider using continuous integration (CI) tools to automate the testing process.

Deployment: Taking Your Application Live

Deployment is the process of making your application accessible to users. It involves taking your code, along with its dependencies and configurations, and placing it on a server that's connected to the internet, allowing users to access it through their web browsers.

Imagine a rocket launch, carefully planned and executed, sending a spacecraft into orbit. Deploying your application is like launching your code into the world, making it available to users and fulfilling its purpose.

We've explored Heroku, a popular cloud platform for deploying web applications, in previous chapters. Heroku provides a convenient and easy-to-use platform for deploying and managing applications. Other deployment options are available:

- **Netlify:** Netlify is a cloud platform that specializes in deploying static websites and web applications. It offers features like continuous deployment, serverless functions, and a global CDN.

- **Vercel:** Vercel is another cloud platform that focuses on deploying front-end applications. It offers similar features to Netlify, along with integrations with popular front-end frameworks like Next.js.

- **AWS:** Amazon Web Services (AWS) offers a comprehensive suite of services for deploying and managing applications, including EC2 (Elastic Compute Cloud) for virtual servers, S3 (Simple Storage Service) for object storage, and more.

- **Azure:** Microsoft Azure is another major cloud platform that provides similar services to AWS.

- **Google Cloud:** Google Cloud Platform (GCP) is Google's cloud computing platform, offering a range of services for deploying and managing applications.

Choose the deployment platform that best aligns with your application's requirements, your budget, and your technical expertise.

Performance Optimization: Ensuring a Smooth User Experience

Performance is a critical aspect of user experience. Users expect web applications to load quickly, respond to interactions smoothly, and provide a seamless experience. Optimizing your application's performance is an ongoing process that involves identifying bottlenecks, analyzing performance metrics, and implementing strategies to improve speed and efficiency.

Imagine a well-maintained car engine, running smoothly and efficiently. Optimizing your application's performance is like fine-tuning your code, reducing friction, maximizing efficiency, and ensuring that it runs smoothly.

Performance optimization in MERN stack applications encompasses various techniques:

- **Caching:** Caching frequently accessed data to reduce the load on your database and back-end.

- **Database Indexing:** Creating indexes on frequently queried fields in your database to speed up query performance.

- **Code Splitting:** Splitting your application code into smaller chunks that can be loaded on demand, reducing the initial loading time.

- **Lazy Loading:** Deferring the loading of non-critical resources, such as images or videos, until they are needed, improving the initial loading time and perceived performance.

- **Image Optimization:** Optimizing images by reducing their file sizes without compromising quality.

- **Minification and Bundling:** Minifying and bundling your JavaScript and CSS files to reduce their size and improve loading times.

- **Server-Side Rendering (SSR):** Rendering your application on the server to improve SEO and perceived performance, especially for the initial page load.

Continuously monitor your application's performance, identify bottlenecks, and implement optimization strategies to ensure a smooth and delightful user experience.

Security: Protecting Your Application and Data

Security is an ongoing concern in web development, and staying informed about potential vulnerabilities and best practices for mitigating them is crucial. Protecting your application and user data is an essential responsibility, and implementing security measures throughout the development process is paramount.

Imagine a well-guarded fortress with multiple layers of defense, protecting its inhabitants from intruders. Security measures act as the fortress walls, safeguarding your application and its data from malicious attacks.

Some key security considerations for MERN stack applications include:

- **Input Validation:** Validate all user input to prevent cross-site scripting (XSS), SQL injection, and other injection attacks.

- **Cross-Site Request Forgery (CSRF) Protection:** Implement CSRF protection to prevent attackers from tricking users into performing unwanted actions.

- **Authentication and Authorization:** Use robust authentication and authorization mechanisms to verify user identities and restrict access to sensitive resources.

- **Secure Password Storage:** Never store passwords in plain text. Use strong hashing algorithms like bcrypt to hash passwords securely.

- **Regular Security Audits:** Conduct regular security audits to identify vulnerabilities and ensure that your security measures are up-to-date.

- **Stay Informed:** Stay informed about the latest security threats and vulnerabilities, and update your dependencies and security practices accordingly.

Security is an ongoing process, and staying vigilant is essential for protecting your application and user data from malicious actors.

Future Trends: Shaping the Horizon of MERN Development

The world of web development is in a constant state of flux, with new technologies, frameworks, and paradigms emerging at a rapid pace. Staying abreast of these trends is essential for building modern and future-proof applications. Here are some future trends that are likely to shape the horizon of MERN stack development:

GraphQL: The Rise of a Powerful Query Language

GraphQL is a query language for APIs and a runtime for fulfilling those queries with your existing data. It provides a more efficient, powerful, and flexible alternative to traditional REST APIs.

Unlike REST APIs, where you often have to make multiple requests to fetch related data, GraphQL allows you to request exactly the data you need in a single query, reducing over-fetching and improving performance.

GraphQL is gaining traction in the MERN stack ecosystem, and its adoption is likely to increase as more developers recognize its benefits.

Serverless: The Shift Towards Infrastructure-Less Development

Serverless computing is continuing to gain momentum, and its impact on web development is becoming increasingly significant. Serverless platforms allow developers to focus on writing code without worrying about the underlying infrastructure, providing scalability, cost-effectiveness, and faster development cycles.

Serverless is likely to become a dominant paradigm for building web applications, especially for applications with variable workloads or infrequent usage.

Micro Frontends: Breaking Down Monoliths

Micro frontends is an architectural style where a front-end application is decomposed into smaller, independent "microapps" that can be developed, deployed, and maintained independently. This approach offers several benefits:

- **Independent Teams:** Different teams can work on different microapps independently, allowing for faster development cycles and greater flexibility.

- **Technology Diversity:** Each microapp can use different technologies, allowing teams to choose the best tools for the job.

- **Incremental Upgrades:** Microapps can be upgraded independently, reducing the risk of large-scale deployments and making it easier to adopt new technologies.

Micro frontends are gaining traction as a way to manage the complexity of large front-end applications, and their adoption is likely to increase as more organizations embrace this architectural style.

WebAssembly (Wasm): Bringing Native Performance to the Web

WebAssembly (Wasm) is a binary instruction format for a stack-based virtual machine. It's designed to be a portable compilation target for programming languages, enabling deployment on the web for client and server applications.

Wasm offers near-native performance, making it suitable for computationally intensive tasks, such as games, image processing, and scientific simulations.

Wasm is still a relatively new technology, but it has the potential to revolutionize web development, bringing native performance to the web and opening up new possibilities for web applications.

Artificial Intelligence (AI) and Machine Learning (ML): Enhancing User Experiences

Artificial Intelligence (AI) and Machine Learning (ML) are transforming various industries, and web development is no exception. AI and ML can be used to enhance user experiences in numerous ways:

- **Personalization:** AI can be used to personalize content, recommendations, and user interfaces based on user behavior and preferences.

- **Chatbots:** AI-powered chatbots can provide automated customer support, answer questions, and guide users through complex processes.

- **Predictive Analytics:** ML can be used to analyze user data and predict future behavior, such as purchase patterns or churn rates.

- **Image and Speech Recognition:** AI-powered image and speech recognition can be used to enhance search, accessibility, and user interactions.

Integrating AI and ML into MERN stack applications can create more intelligent, personalized, and engaging user experiences.

Progressive Web Apps (PWAs): Bridging the Gap Between Web and Native

Progressive Web Apps (PWAs) are web applications that offer a native-app-like experience. They can be installed on a user's device, work offline, and access device features, such as push notifications and camera access.

PWAs offer several benefits over traditional web apps:

- **Improved Performance:** PWAs can be cached on the user's device, providing faster loading times and a smoother experience.

- **Offline Access:** PWAs can work offline, allowing users to access content even when they don't have an internet connection.

- **Native-like Features:** PWAs can access device features, providing a more integrated and engaging experience.

Building PWAs using the MERN stack can provide a more engaging and app-like experience for your users, bridging the gap between web and native applications.

The Metaverse: A New Frontier for Web Experiences

The metaverse is a collective virtual shared space, created by the convergence of virtually enhanced physical reality and physically persistent virtual space, including the sum of all virtual worlds, augmented reality, and the internet. It's still an early concept, but it has the potential to revolutionize how we interact with the web, creating immersive and interactive experiences.

The MERN stack, with its ability to build dynamic and interactive web applications, is well-positioned to play a role in shaping the metaverse. As the metaverse evolves, we can expect to see innovative applications built using the MERN stack that leverage virtual reality, augmented reality, and other emerging technologies to create engaging and immersive web experiences.

As you embark on your journey of building MERN stack applications, remember that the world of web development is a constantly evolving landscape. Embrace best practices to ensure code quality, maintainability, and scalability. Stay informed about future trends, experiment with new technologies, and adapt your skills to the ever-changing demands of the web development world. With a solid foundation in the MERN stack and a forward-looking mindset, you're well-equipped to create exceptional web experiences that meet the needs of today's users and shape the future of the web.

www.ingramcontent.com/pod-product-compliance
Lightning Source LLC
Chambersburg PA
CBHW070931050326
40689CB00014B/3166